Resting in
GOD'S
SOVEREIGNTY

Resting in
GOD'S
SOVEREIGNTY

A 30-Day Devotional on
God's Plan for His People

ERNEST EASLEY

PUBLISHING
BRENTWOOD, TENNESSEE

Published by B&H Publishing Group
Brentwood, Tennessee

Dewey Decimal Classification: 231.5
Subject Heading: PROVIDENCE AND GOVERNMENT
OF GOD / GOD / FAITH

Cover design by Brian Bobel.
Illustration of Glencoe, Scotland by T. B. Howard,
1874, sourced from duncan1890/iStock.
Author photo by Stephen Beasley.

1 2 3 4 5 6 • 28 27 26 25 24

It is a joy to dedicate this devotional book to the two women in my life God has used to teach me more about resting in God's sovereignty. To my wife Julie, whose deep faith has helped develop and deepen my faith. To my mother, Billie Sue Easley, whose prayer life has challenged mine.

ACKNOWLEDGMENTS

I want to thank my good friend David Marr, who is always ready to assist me in proofing my manuscripts. He is such a great encourager and friend. I'm also grateful for my editor at B&H Publishing, Logan Pyron, whose encouragement and support helped turn this dream into a reality.

FOREWORD

*L*ord, though I didn't see this coming I know you did. I know this didn't catch you by surprise. Knowing you are sovereign and that nothing can get to me without first coming through you, thank you for this cancer. Now use it for your glory and my good."

Those were the words I heard my father pray, with his hands extended to the sky, just moments after telling our family that he didn't know if he was going to live or die. It was a moment that none of us will ever forget . . . and one that took my personal journey of trusting God and resting in his sovereignty to an entirely new level.

As our family navigated that season, those words echoed in my ears: "Knowing you are sovereign . . . Knowing that nothing can get to me without first coming through you . . ."

As a nineteen-year-old young man, it led me to ask the question: What does it mean that God is sovereign? And can I really trust God in his sovereignty?

In the dictionary, the word *sovereign* is connected to words like "great" or "superior" or being "supreme in authority." But what I came to realize was that God's sovereignty was far greater than that. When you reference God's sovereignty, you're basically acknowledging that God is in complete control of all things and at all times.

If you are a Christ-follower and you believe your Bible is true, it's abundantly clear that God has always been, and will always be, in charge. Psalm 135:6 says, "The LORD does whatever he pleases in heaven and on earth, in the seas and all the depths."

That verse gives us an amazing picture of God's power and control. It shows us that God is the ultimate authority in every single territory, and nothing that happens in this life or on this earth, takes him by surprise. Colossians 1:16–17 tells us, "all things have been created through him and for him. He is before all things, and by him all things hold together."

That verse says that God is our creator, but it also shows that he's our sustainer; the one that holds all things together. And it should be comforting for us to know that God's approval process in allowing things to happen or preventing things from happening is contingent on his perfect plan.

Now, does that make sense to us? No. Very rarely does that make sense. How could terrible things be a part of a greater plan? How can a cancer diagnosis, a deadly car accident, or a child dying in the womb be a part of God's greater plan? Most of us will die one day, and we'll still be scratching our heads, asking the question, "Why?"

As human beings, we will most likely never have a perspective that can justify a loving God approving such terrible things, but hopefully as you make this thirty-day journey of learning to rest in God's sovereignty, you'll discover, like

I have, . . . that most of the time, our lack of rest (fears) is directly connected to our lack of trust (faith). And our lack of trust is typically the result of our limited perspective.

Our vision and our perspectives are very different from God's vision and God's perspective. We see to the corner, but we serve a God who sees around the corner. We're watching the movie of our life play out, frame-by-frame, but our God knows how the movie of our life ends, and ultimately, the Bible says in Isaiah 55 that His plans are far greater than our plans.

Trusting God is easy when times are good; when we're healthy and happy, prosperous and protected. Trusting God is easy in seasons like these. But how do we rest in his sovereignty when we don't understand his plan? My prayer is that over these next thirty days, God will answer that question in your heart and equip you to rest in him in every season and in every circumstance in your remaining time here on earth.

—Jordan Easley

Often, when our world begins to fall apart in front of our eyes, our faith becomes shaken, and we can find ourselves doubting the goodness and sovereignty of God. As a seventeen-year-old boy, I (Jonah) found myself there. As I went to my room to process what I had just learned in a family meeting, I was fearful, angry, and confused. My dad had just told us that he had fast-growing cancer inside his body and didn't know if he would live or die. In one moment, my confidence and trust in God were forced to move from an ideological framework into a real-world crisis that would expose my actual belief. Adrian Rogers famously said, "A faith that hasn't been tested can't be trusted."[1] For me, this was one of those tests that tested my genuine trust in God.

Through tears, an endless list of "what-if" questions filled my mind. *Is God still in control? If He is, what could possibly be doing? Is He perfect and trustworthy?* Amid that thought overload, my dad walked into my room to check on me. He was the one with cancer, and he was checking on me! He knew this would significantly impact all of our lives. But at that moment, I found a calming assurance in my dad's demeanor. No panic. No fear. Just a trusting belief that whatever God allows into his life is good. His faith helped to strengthen mine as we began walking through a tough battle as a family.

Over the years, I have witnessed my dad's example of dependence on God and a supernatural trust in his sovereignty. From difficult ministry seasons, relational challenges, and fighting for his life, my dad has been a great example of relying on the promises, power, and presence of Jesus in the storms of life. It's easy to say Jesus is loving and kind when the waters are calm. But when the diagnosis comes and life seems to be falling apart, believing Jesus is loving and trustworthy can become more challenging. When the storms of life come, which they always do, we have the assurance that rough waters in life can lead to a deeper relationship with Jesus.

My dad's example shows me that every storm is a new opportunity to examine who you believe Jesus to be and where you have placed your faith. Even when the waters aren't smooth, we can stand on the promise of God's presence. So no matter the outcome, we can have peace in the storm. Watching my dad endure great storms has been an example worthy of emulating. He's helped others learn, as Malcolm Muggeridge said, "Everything that has truly enhanced and enlighted my existence has been through affliction. . . ."[2] It's counterintuitive, but usually our most significant trials are what mold and shape us most. Christ alone is our refuge and gives us hope through any storm, test, or diagnosis. He is Lord of all, loves us, and is always with us. Thanks, Dad, for showing me how to walk in this way.

—Jonah Easley

DAY 1

I have learned to be content in whatever
circumstances I find myself.

PHILIPPIANS 4:11

Today's Focus: Paul resting in God's sovereignty.

Today's Insight: Resting in God's
sovereignty is personal.

What's the first thing that comes to mind when you hear the word *sovereignty*? Many have likely heard the word, but *knowing* what it means, is something else. Often, whenever people hear about the sovereignty of God, they think of it as rigid, like a huge iron vice holding everything in a tight grip. But we're going to discover over these next thirty days that God's sovereignty never tramples on the free will of man. Yes, man is free, but God is sovereign. There is no incompatibility between divine sovereignty and human will.[3]

What does the sovereignty of God mean? It means that God possesses all power and is ruler of all things. Look at the word *sovereignty*. What word do you see in the middle of it? *Reign*. To say that God is sovereign is to say that God reigns.

Did you know God declares himself sovereign? We hear him saying in Isaiah 43:15: "I am the LORD, your Holy One, the Creator of Israel, your King." We hear David declaring God's sovereignty in his prayer in 1 Chronicles 29:12: "Riches and honor come from you, and you are the ruler of everything. Power and might are in your hand, and it is in your hand to make great and to give strength to all." We hear Jehoshaphat declaring in his prayer in 2 Chronicles 20:6: "LORD, God of our ancestors, are you not the God who is in heaven, and do you not rule over all the kingdoms of the nations?"

Listen to David in Psalm 103:19: "The LORD has established his throne in heaven, and his kingdom rules over all." Do you know what his "kingdom" includes? It includes everything! He rules over everything, which includes your life, your circumstances, your challenges, and yes, even over your crises.

Let me ask you this: Who rules over a kingdom? A king. Right? So, when we talk about God being sovereign, we're talking about God being King. In fact, this word *kingdom* refers to royal power or dominion.

Learn this today: his is an absolute monarchy! Proverbs 16:4: "The LORD has prepared everything for his purpose." Psalm 97:1: "The LORD reigns!" Our God is sovereign! Even the pagan sailors on the boat with Jonah acknowledged his sovereignty when they called out to the Lord in Jonah 1:14, "For you, LORD, have done just as you pleased."

Abraham Kuyper was spot-on when he wrote: "There is not one square inch of the entire creation about which Jesus Christ does not cry out, 'This is mine! This belongs to me.'"[4]

Now, it's one thing to *know* that God is sovereign; it's another thing to *rest* in his sovereignty. It comes down to perspective. It's like that Jewish man in Hungary who went to his rabbi, complaining, "Life is unbearable. There are nine of us living in one room. What can I do?" The rabbi answered, "Take your goat into the room with you and come back in one week."

A week later the man returned looking more distraught than before. "We can't stand it," he told the rabbi. "The goat is filthy." The rabbi said, "Go home and let the goat out, and come back in one week."

A week later the man returned, radiant and excited, and said, "Rabbi! Life is wonderful! We enjoy every minute of it now that there's no goat, only the nine of us."[5] Perspective helps, doesn't it?

If anyone understood perspective, it was the apostle Paul. While sitting in a Roman prison, we hear him say in Philippians 4:11, "I have learned to be content in whatever circumstances I find myself."

Here's a secret we all should know: the secret of being content! The key is found in verse 13: "I am able to do all things through him who strengthens me." That verse tells us contentment starts from within and then works its way out. In other words, contentment is an inside job. The secret to contentment is not a what; it's a who. Jesus is the secret. Through Jesus we can rest in God's sovereignty.

Listen to those words again: "*I* have learned to be content" (v. 11, emphasis added). Resting in God's sovereignty is personal. In the Greek language, the word translated "I" is written as a strong emphatic. In other words, the emphasis in this verse is on the word "I." "*I* have learned" (emphasis added). Resting in God's sovereignty is something we must learn for ourselves. It is personal. Nobody can learn it for you except you.

So, how do we learn it? The same way Paul learned it. We must be teachable. Are you teachable, or does your pride keep you from learning? Are you impressed with being a know-it-all? Don't be! The more I learn, the more I realize how much I have to learn. That's why I'm always learning and asking God to help me remain teachable.

Resting in God's sovereignty is personal. I can no more rest in God's sovereignty for you anymore than Paul could rest in God's sovereignty for the believers in Philippi. I must learn to rest in his sovereignty for me. You must learn to rest in his sovereignty for you. Therefore, stay teachable.

Are you resting in God's sovereignty today? There's not a more peaceful place to live than in his sovereignty. It will be a great day in your life when you learn that resting in God's sovereignty will liberate your life. Charles Spurgeon said, "The sovereignty of God is the pillow on which the Christian lays his head."[6]

Today's Prayer: *Lord, teach me to rest in your sovereignty. In Jesus's name, amen.*

I have learned to be content in whatever
circumstances I find myself.
PHILIPPIANS 4:11

Today's Focus: Paul resting in God's sovereignty.

Today's Insight: Resting in God's
sovereignty is progressive.

As you got out of bed this morning, you woke up in a world being ruled by God. He ruled yesterday. He rules today. He will rule tomorrow. Here is how God said it in Revelation 1:8: "'I am the Alpha and the Omega,' says the Lord God, 'the one who is, who was, and who is to come,'" and then, almost like a second thought, he says, "the Almighty."

The word *almighty* comes from a Greek compound word meaning "all power." The nearest English translation of it is "all-sovereign."[7] It's noteworthy that this word is never used for any being other than God himself. He alone is all-sovereign! He alone is all-mighty!

So the question again is: How do we rest in his sovereignty?

Today we learn from Paul that resting in God's sovereignty is *progressive*. In other words, it is learned gradually, over time, not overnight.

> I have *learned* to be content. (v. 11, emphasis
> added)

Do you remember when you first started learning math? I can still remember my first-grade teacher handing out math problems on a piece of paper for us to take home to practice. That was before the modern-day printers we have today. Back then they used a mimeograph machine, which was a duplicating machine that produced copies from a stencil and an ink roller. I can still almost smell the ink!

I've always struggled with math. I remember when I finally learned how to add and subtract and then to multiply and divide. Once I learned how, I knew it! You could wake me up from a dead sleep and ask, "Ernest, what is eight times four?" I could tell you it's thirty-two! And then go back to sleep in minutes.

Once I learned it, it stuck! It's the same with resting in God's sovereignty. When Paul says, "I have learned to be content," the Greek word he uses that's translated "learned" is *emathon*. Try saying it out loud: *e-math-on*. In the middle of this Greek word is the English four-letter word: *math*. Paul had learned to rest in God's sovereignty like we learned the multiplication chart. Once he learned it, he knew it. The same is true for us.

Now that raises the question: How did Paul learn to be content in all circumstances? What was his learning process? You might say, "Ernest, I'm not sure. Besides, even if I knew it, I'm not sure I could ever get there." Yes, you can! You can learn to rest in God's sovereignty, or as Paul described it, you can "be content in whatever circumstances [you] find [yourself]." And if you're unsure about that, I can tell you why you can be. When Paul said, "I have learned to be content," that tells me there was a time when he hadn't learned this; there was a day when he did not know how to rest in God's sovereignty. If he had to learn it, that means there was a day he didn't know it, and that gives us all hope.

In 1998, I battled for my life. I had a fast-growing malignant cancer in my throat, and I underwent forty-four radiation treatments to extend my life. Since then, I've had several issues caused from long-term radiation damage. The most recent issue is scar tissue buildup reducing my swallowing and speaking. It's nearly impossible for me to swallow food or to teach or preach. Someone asked me what God has been teaching me through this latest issue. Here's what I told him:

God is teaching me to rest in his sovereignty.

I'm not sure I can say with Paul, "I have learned," but I can say, "I am learning." Perhaps like you, I'm still in the process of learning to rest in God's sovereignty. Honestly, I've accepted my circumstances. What makes my struggles okay is knowing that God is using them to help teach me to rest in his sovereignty. Don't feel sorry for me. Frankly, I feel sorry for you if you haven't learned the peace that comes from resting in his sovereignty. I would rather struggle with speaking and swallowing and learn to rest in his sovereignty than to have no struggles without having learned to rest in his sovereignty.

So, how did Paul learn it? How do we learn it? You can't learn it from reading a book or by attending a conference or by hearing a sermon or by attending a small group. These may help you get there, but I'm finding that God usually uses three tools to help us learn to rest in his sovereignty:

Time, Troubles, and Trust

The tool of *time*. As with math, you don't learn it overnight. It requires time.

The tool of *troubles*. Paul learned the importance of this tool through seclusion, struggles, and suffering. Since you're not going to avoid troubles, you might as well decide not to waste them but rather to invest them. Through the troubles we face, we learn to rest in his sovereignty.

The tool of *trust*. Resting requires trust, trusting God to use your troubles to help conform you into the image of his Son and to fulfill his purposes.

The children of Israel never learned to trust God. God couldn't do enough miracles to gain their trust. Let me ask you this: How much more does God have to do in your life to gain your trust? One more miracle? One more prayer answered? One more _____? You fill in the blank.

If Paul had to learn it, we all must as well: his sovereignty is trustworthy.

Today's Prayer: *Lord, give me the faith to get to the place in my relationship with you to honestly say that you do not have to do one more thing in my life for me to trust you. In Jesus's name, amen.*

—————

I have learned to be content in whatever
circumstances I find myself.
Philippians 4:11

Today's Focus: Paul resting in God's sovereignty.

Today's Insight: Resting in God's
sovereignty requires persistence.

D o you have tenacity? Do you refuse to give up or let go? Perhaps you're familiar with the story of the optimistic frog. It goes like this:

> Two frogs fell into a deep cream bowl,
> One was an optimistic soul;
> But the other took the gloomy view,

"We shall drown," he cried, without
    more ado.
So with a last despairing cry,
He flung up his legs and he said,
"Good-bye."

Quoth the other frog with a merry grin,
    "I can't get out, but I won't give in.
I'll just swim around till my strength is
    spent,
Then will I die the more content."
Bravely he swam till it would seem
His struggles began to churn the cream.
On the top of the butter at last he stopped,
And out of the bowl he gaily hopped.
What of the moral? 'Tis easily found:
If you can't hop out, keep swimming
    round.[8]

Without persistence or tenacity, you will never learn the joy of resting in God's sovereignty. As Jimmy Draper once said, "Don't quit before you finish." So, where does that inner drive come from that keeps us in the saddle when the horse we're riding starts to buck? What gave Paul the tenacity not to quit, to push through his challenges and reach the point of saying, "I have learned *to be content in whatever circumstances I find myself*" (emphasis added)?

What does he mean by "content"? How did that happen in his life? More important, how do we, like Paul, become "content in whatever circumstances" we find ourselves?

The Greek word translated "content" has several shades of meaning. It comes from a word meaning "to suffice." It's used in 2 Corinthians 9:8 where it's translated "having everything you need" or, more literally, "self-sufficiency." It speaks of having enough.

The *Thayer's Lexicon* defines it as "possessing enough to need to aid or support."[9] *The New Linguistic and Exegetical Key to the Greek New Testament* says, "The word indicates independence of external circumstances and often means of the state of one who supports himself without aid from others."[10]

Let me see if I can put this all together so we can understand what it means to be "content." When Paul said, "I have learned to be content in whatever circumstances I find myself," he was saying, "I have learned to be self-sufficient." You say, "That doesn't sound right. In fact, it sounds a little arrogant and humanistic." Then let me try again to clear it up. How about this: "I have everything within me to be content. I don't depend on anything on the outside to satisfy me. I carry my own sufficiency with me on the inside."

Still confused? Then let me ask you this: What inner sufficiency did Paul possess that enabled him to be content in all his circumstances or to rest in God's sovereignty? It was the presence and peace of Jesus Christ living in him!

His circumstances didn't bring him contentment, but Christ in him did. Here's how Paul said it in 1 Timothy 6:6:

"But godliness with contentment is great gain." Do you see it? It wasn't any outside assistant that brought him contentment; it was his inside assistant who brought him contentment: Jesus! With Jesus living within him, he had everything he needed for contentment.

Do you know what contentment really is? As someone once said, "It's not getting what you want, but wanting what you already have. Contentment will make a poor man rich. And discontentment will make a rich man poor."

Sometimes it is God's grace that we don't receive what we think we want. I once read about two tears who met up along the river of life. One tear said to the other, "Where did you come from?" "Oh," the second tear said, "I'm the tear of a girl who loved a man and lost him. And where did you come from?" The first tear answered, "I'm the tear of the girl who found him and married him."

What did Paul possess that no longer required any external circumstances to be content in all his circumstances? The answer and secret are found in Philippians 4:13: "I am able to do all things through him who strengthens me." Do you see it? Contentment or resting in God's sovereignty is something you learn if you don't quit too soon and then live. Your circumstances reveal your contentment.

When I was told I had a fast-growing malignant cancer in my throat, I remember praying one day, *Lord, I know nothing can get to me without first going through you. I know you're not caught off guard by this. You've been preparing me for forty years to fight this battle. So I thank you for the cancer. I know you're going to use it in my life for good and for your glory. I know I'm in your hands. However this turns out, I trust you.*

In that moment, I know that I was resting in God's sovereignty. I had everything I needed within me—namely, Jesus Christ—to rest or be content. Again, your circumstances reveal your contentment.

Are you resting in or resisting God's sovereignty? You say, "How do I know if I'm resting or resisting God's sovereignty?" Here's how:

- Resting in God's sovereignty produces peace.
- Resisting God's sovereignty produces worry.

And let me add that your resting in or resisting his sovereignty doesn't alter his sovereignty. Fighting him or having faith in him doesn't change his sovereignty. Let me say it another way.

- Running toward his sovereignty leads to contentment.
- Running away from his sovereignty leads to discontentment.

Paul learned the secret to living in contentment was surrendering to God's sovereignty. Listen to him again in Philippians 4:12–13: "In any and all circumstances I have learned the secret of being content—whether well fed or hungry, whether in abundance or in need. I am able to do all things through him who strengthens me."

If I were going to take a picture of resting in God's sovereignty, here's how it would look:

- peace, not panic
- calm, not conflicted
- trusting, not troubled
- faith, not fear
- resting, not restless

Are you resting in or resisting the sovereignty of God? The way to get more of God is for God to get more of you! The more God gets of you, the more you get of God. Here's more good news:

First, resting in his sovereignty is the secret to living a satisfied life.

Second, if you are redeemed, you can rest!

Do you have health issues? If you're redeemed, you can rest!

Do you have challenging circumstances? If you're redeemed, you can rest!

Do you not have all the answers? If you're redeemed, you can rest!

You will never experience the rest found in God's sovereignty without being redeemed. Redemption is found at the cross of Jesus, who bled and died, was buried, and then arose from the dead on the third day, making redemption available to you.

Let the redeemed learn to rest in God's sovereignty!

Today's Prayer: *Lord, thank you for redeeming me through your Son, my Savior, the Lord Jesus Christ. Remind me today that, through him, I can rest! In Jesus's name, amen.*

David spoke the words of this song to the
LORD on the day the LORD rescued him.

2 SAMUEL 22:1

Today's Focus: David inspired by God's sovereignty.

Today's Insight: God's sovereignty has great depth.

Who hasn't been inspired by someone or some event to do something they would have never tried without that inspiration? The *Oxford Advanced American Dictionary* defines *inspiration* as "the process that takes place when somebody sees or hears something that causes them to have exciting new ideas or makes them want to create something, especially in art, music or literature."[11]

My earliest memory of being inspired to try something I had never done before was when I was seven years old. Our family had seen the movie *Mary Poppins*, and I left the theater that day inspired by her ability to fly holding on to an umbrella.

When we arrived back home, I found an umbrella, climbed on top of our house, held on tight to the umbrella, and jumped, believing the umbrella would slowly take me to the ground like Mary Poppins. I was wrong! I dropped to the ground like a rock! I learned a hard lesson that day: be careful of who or what inspires you. If you're not careful, the inspiration you receive could result in a fall.

Perhaps your mother or grandmother inspired you to cook.

Perhaps a parent inspired you to try sports.

Perhaps a teacher inspired you to become a teacher.

Perhaps a coach inspired you to achieve in athletics or to become a coach.

Inspiration is a game changer and life changer. Most of us would not be where we are today without someone or something inspiring us to achieve and accomplish and even acquire what we have and are today. Thank God for the inspirers that have crossed our paths.

We all need inspiration to accomplish great things, including King David. David was more than just a great leader;

he was a great hunter and warrior. A true man's man. You wouldn't think a man like that would also be a great musician, but he was. And like every musician who produces songs, David needed inspiration.

Behind the words of every song, spiritual or secular, you will find an inspired writer. There's always a story behind every song. Sometimes songs are written out of life's tragedies. At other times songs are written out of life's triumphs. But the one thing they all have in common is inspiration.

This devotional book is a good example of that. This book was born in my heart from a period of great physical struggle from long-term radiation damage to my throat, restricting my swallowing and speaking. When asked what God was teaching me through it, my response was: "God is teaching me to rest in his sovereignty." That lesson drove me back to God's Word to discover how Bible characters rested in and responded to God's sovereignty. The result? Inspiration! And what inspired David to write the song recorded in 2 Samuel 22 and also inspired me to write this devotional book? It was the sovereignty of God! His sovereignty is inspiring.

Yes! David was inspired to write the words of this song because of God's sovereignty. My prayer for you during this journey is to discover how the sovereignty of God can become an inspiration for you to do something with your life that will both outlive you and give glory to God. After thousands of years, we're still reading David's song of thanksgiving that both outlived him and continues to give God glory.

We read in verse 1: "David spoke the words of this song to the LORD on the day the LORD rescued him from the grasp of all his enemies and from the grasp of Saul." Being a musician, what probably started out as speaking for David soon turned into singing the words of this song to the Lord.

Notice when the inspiration came for David to write this song. We read in verse 1: "On the day the LORD rescued him." Not one day later. Not one week later. Not one year later. But "on the day the LORD rescued him." David wasted no time in writing this song. His heart was so full of gratitude he couldn't hold it in. That's how inspiration works, isn't it? It invades our life when we least expect it. David recognized his moment of inspiration and moved on it.

Notice in verses 2–3 *the depth of God's sovereignty in his life*: "The LORD is my rock, my fortress, and my deliverer, my God, my rock where I seek refuge. My shield, the horn of my salvation, my stronghold, my refuge, and my Savior, you save me from violence." Did you notice how personal God's sovereignty was in his life? *My* rock. *My* fortress. *My* deliverer. *My* God. *My* rock. *My* shield. *My* stronghold. *My* refuge. And then finally, *my* Savior.

David had learned when times got hard that the Lord was sovereign and his only security. Have you ever wondered what keeps God so faithful to you, especially during difficult days? The answer is found in verse 20, where David said, "He brought me out to a spacious place; he rescued me because he delighted in me." Do you know that God delights in you? He delights in me. God takes pleasure in us.

Learn this today: because God is sovereign, you are secure. Therefore, rest in his sovereignty. Because God is sovereign, he is your rock, your fortress, your deliverer, your shield, your salvation, your stronghold, your refuge, and yes, your Savior!

Celebrate it today! Confess it today! Cherish it today: our Savior is sovereign! We can say along with the psalmist today, "This God, our God forever and ever—he will always lead us" (Ps. 48:14).

Today's Prayer: *Lord, we acknowledge your sovereignty over our life. Therefore, we know that nothing can get to us without first going through you. We trust you for our eternity. Help us to trust you with the here and now. You are my rock, my refuge, my shield, and my Savior. In Jesus's name, amen.*

DAY 5

LORD, you are my lamp; the LORD
illuminates my darkness.

2 SAMUEL 22:29

Today's Focus: David inspired by God's sovereignty.

Today's Insight: We can delight in God's sovereignty.

What do you delight in? What brings you great pleasure and joy? If you were to write down the top five things that delight you or give you pleasure, what would you include on your list? Take a moment and write them down. You could label them: *The Five Top Things that Bring Me the Most Pleasure in Life.*

So, what made your list? Perhaps your family made the list. Perhaps an accomplishment such as your business or athletics, perhaps playing an instrument or swimming or painting on a canvas, or outdoor activities such as camping or hunting or fishing. I suppose there are as many answers as there are people.

I wonder what would have made King David's list. Perhaps winning a battle or conquering another enemy brought him delight. Had I been David, that is what would have made my top-five list. What about delighting in the writing of another psalm and then singing it to the Lord? Certainly, a top five. At some point in his life, Bathsheba made his top-five list, which should caution us about what or who makes our list.

Whatever we treasure inspires us to action. That's why we need to be careful about what makes our list, because what we delight in or take pleasure in will soon consume and control us. Look at your list. Does anything on your list drive you away from God? Are there things on your list that drive you to God? These questions may cause you to rethink your list.

As with David, our lists are constantly changing. Some things that were on my *pleasure list* in my twenties have now been replaced in my sixties. One thing you must appreciate about David was that he never quit.

When you get to 2 Samuel 22, David was an older man yet still battling. Chapter 21 records several battles involving David against his archenemies the Philistines. He won every battle. Then, chapter 22 begins with these words in verse 1: "David spoke the words of this song to the Lord on the day the Lord rescued him from the grasp of all his enemies and from the grasp of Saul." And then beginning in verse 2, David reveals one of the items that made his top-five list during that season of his life: the sovereignty of God. Don't miss this: David delighted in the sovereignty of God!

Can I ask you some personal questions? Has God's sovereignty brought delight and pleasure into your life? Are you delighting in the sovereignty of God? Here's what I've discovered: until God's sovereignty breaks into your top five, you will never rest in his sovereignty.

Woven throughout David's song, we find him delighting in God's sovereignty. Here are a few ways:

- He delighted in God's power. Verses 17–18: "He reached down from on high and took hold of me; he pulled me out of deep water. He rescued me from my powerful enemy and from those who hated me."
- He delighted in God's support. Verse 19: "They [my enemies] confronted me in the day of my calamity, but the LORD was my support."
- He delighted in God's faithfulness. Verse 26: "With the faithful you prove yourself faithful."
- He delighted in God's light. Verse 29: "LORD, you are my lamp; the LORD illuminates my darkness."

- He delighted in God's Word. Verse 31: "God—his way is perfect; the word of the LORD is pure."
- He delighted in God's support. Verse 37: "You make a spacious place beneath me for my steps, and my ankles do not give way."

As he concludes his song, he declares in verse 50: "Therefore I will give thanks to you among the nations, LORD; I will sing praise about your name." And then he declares his delight for God's loyalty in verse 51: "He is a tower of salvation for his king; he shows loyalty to his anointed, to David and his descendants forever."

Don't let the truth of God's sovereignty confound or confuse or concern you; let it compel you as it did David. You may not express your delight in God's sovereignty in writing a song, but you could express it through serving, giving, or sharing your God story with others. That's what David did through his song: he shared his God story with others.

Don't miss this! Recognizing God's sovereignty didn't impair him; it inspired him. It inspired him to write a song that never would have been written otherwise. He realized God was working behind the scenes to do a work through him and for him. That's true for us too. Because God is sovereign, he's always working even when we don't see him working. You ask, "Ernest, how can I know that's true in my life?" Because God is sovereign.

Let's conclude today's devotional with a deeper look at verse 29 where David sings, "LORD, you are my lamp; the LORD illuminates my darkness." Can't you see David, the warrior with battle wounds and cuts on his face and arms, praying repeatedly, "LORD, you are my lamp," and then taking a deep breath, slowly letting the air flow out of his lungs and acknowledging, "The LORD illuminates my darkness."

Looking back over some of his darkest hours, he realized God had been the lamp to light his way. You don't have to look back far to see how God has lighted your path. I remember having to make some critical life-and-death decisions and thinking, *If I make the wrong decision here, it could cost me my life.* All I could do was trust God in the moment to illuminate my darkness. And from that trust, I discovered a genuine delight in the sovereignty of God.

David was given enough light to see God at work in his life: "LORD, you are my lamp" (v. 29). If you take a lamp or lantern into the woods at night, you won't be able to see all the trees in the forest, but you will see far enough to keep your footing sure. Here's the delight of God's sovereignty: he gives you enough light on your path to help guide your steps.

Today's Prayer: *Lord, thank you for your work in my life. As I delight today in your sovereignty, inspire me to accomplish something for you that will impact the lives of others. In Jesus's name, amen.*

DAY 6

He frees me from my enemies.

2 SAMUEL 22:49

Today's Focus: David inspired by God's sovereignty.

Today's Insight: God's sovereignty
delivers in life's interruptions.

Who likes interruptions? They always come at the wrong time. I was recently flying from Chattanooga, Tennessee, to Midland/Odessa, Texas. I had to fly from Chattanooga to Dallas/Fort Worth for the first leg of my flight. Then I changed planes in Dallas to catch a forty-five-minute flight to Midland/Odessa. What could go wrong? Right?

The flight to Dallas went off without a hitch. In fact, I had nearly a two-hour layover, giving me time to eat something before flying to Midland/Odessa. I was relaxing and enjoying a meal, and thought I'd check the flight schedule to make sure my flight was still boarding at the designated gate. When I pulled up the information on my phone, there it was in bold print: FLIGHT CANCELLED. I thought, *How could that be? It's just a forty-five-minute flight!*

I went to the ticket counter for assistance. They explained my flight was cancelled but I could fly standby on the next flight. I asked them two questions: "First, is that flight full, and second, how many are currently on standby?" You guessed it. The flight was full, and I'd be sixth on the standby list. I looked at them and asked, "I'm not getting on that plane, am I?" They said, "Probably not, but we can put you up in a hotel for the night and give you a $12 food voucher." I said, "I suppose I don't have a choice." I was told to go downstairs and retrieve my luggage and call the hotel for shuttle service.

When I went to retrieve my luggage, I was informed that since my flight was cancelled, they put it on the next flight (the one for which I was on standby) and it would arrive in Midland/Odessa before I would. No flight and no luggage. Then I thought, *But at least I have a comfortable hotel to sleep in tonight.* I was wrong! After arriving, I soon discovered the hotel was being renovated. The lobby was torn apart. The restaurant was closed so they had provided a food truck outside. The room smelled of paint thinner. To make it even worse, I couldn't figure out how to work the television. It was a disaster. There I was, no luggage, no restaurant, and now, no entertainment to, at least, pass the time.

I survived the night and made my flight the next morning. As I sat on the plane, it occurred to me that it took longer for me to fly from Chattanooga to Midland/Odessa than it did for me to fly from Chattanooga to Israel the previous month! You've got to love unexpected interruptions!

Yes, even life interruptions are from God. If "all things work together for the good of those who love God, who are called according to his purpose" (Rom. 8:28), that includes what we call and consider "interruptions." I find the words of Oswald Chambers helpful: "I take interruptions as from the Lord. They belong in my schedule because the schedule is God's to arrange at His pleasure."[12]

What often appears to us as an interruption is God fulfilling his plans and purposes. You know, his sovereignty. The Bible tells us in Ephesians 2:10: "For we are his workmanship, created in Christ Jesus for good works, which God prepared ahead of time for us to do." That includes what we call "interruptions."

God interrupted Philip while experiencing revival in Samaria and sent him to the desert. That interruption resulted in an Ethiopian man's being saved and taking the gospel to another continent. What started out as an apparent interruption to Philip was a part of God's plan from the start. For Philip it was an interruption. For God it was an intention.

King David's life was filled with what appeared to be interruptions. He was constantly being interrupted by the foul play of Saul, the godless Philistines, or some other enemy. We need to learn what David learned: what appears as an interruption to us is just another opportunity for God to show us his glory and power. After all, that's what resting in his sovereignty is all about, isn't it?

The song David spoke to the Lord on the day he was rescued "from the grasp of all his enemies and from the grasp of Saul" (2 Sam. 22:1) reveals a lot about David and the Lord. Reflecting on God's sovereignty inspired him to script and speak and probably later sing this song expressing the deliverance of God's sovereignty. Learn this today: God's sovereignty is filled with deliverances for his children. He has a deliverance for every disaster. He has a provision for every problem. He has a purpose for every pain. He has a plan for every predicament.

We hear David saying in 2 Samuel 22:49, "He frees me from my enemies." How would David have experienced that freeing power of God's sovereignty had he not had enemies?

We hear David saying in 2 Samuel 22:18, "He rescued me from my powerful enemy and from those who hated me." How would David have experienced the rescuing power of God's sovereignty had he not been hated by his enemies?

David added in Psalm 34:17: "The righteous cry out, and the LORD hears, and rescues them from all their troubles." How could he say that? Again, because he had experienced the rescuing power of God's sovereignty.

We hear David saying in 2 Samuel 22:17, "He reached down from on high and took hold of me; he pulled me out of deep water." How would David have experienced the saving power of God's sovereignty had he not been in deep water?

It's no wonder he wraps up his song in 2 Samuel 22:47: "The LORD lives—blessed be my rock! God, the rock of my salvation, is exalted." And then in verse 50: "Therefore I will give thanks to you among the nations, LORD; I will sing praises about your name."

The deliverance of God's sovereignty helps inspire us to live on mission with him. Take a moment to reflect on his many deliverances in your life. How he's "reached down from on high and took hold of [*you*]" and then "pulled [*you*] out of deep water" (v. 17). It's inspiring, isn't it? It inspired David to write this song. What about you? How will God's many deliverances inspire you? One last thing to keep in mind today: with every deliverance comes a greater trust. I could say it this way: every time he delivers us, our trust in him grows.

Today's Prayer: *Lord, thank you for the many times you've reached down and taken hold of me and delivered me out of deep water. May your many deliverances inspire me to live on mission with you today. Teach me to rest in your sovereignty. In Jesus's name, amen.*

———————

DAY 7

*"If the God we serve exists, then he can
rescue us from the furnace of blazing fire."*
Daniel 3:17

Today's Focus: The three young Hebrew
men and God's sovereignty.

Today's Insight: Godly companions are essential.

D o you rest well at night? There's just nothing better to
refresh and revive you than a good night's sleep. It's common knowledge that rest is vital for better mental health,
increased concentration and memory, a healthier immune
system, reduced stress, improved mood, and even a better
metabolism. If you don't believe it, just try going a few days
without sleep!

I recently had a medical procedure which required my being put to sleep. After being prepped and rolled into the surgery room, the last thing I heard the anesthesiologist (the one who puts you to sleep) say to me was, "Mr. Easley, enjoy your rest."

It's only fitting on this seventh day of our journey to consider what it means to *rest* in God's sovereignty. We read in Genesis 2:2 that "On the seventh day God had completed his work that he had done, and he rested on the seventh day from all the work that he had done." Even God rested. The word translated *rested* means "to stop, to cease, or to be at a standstill." God stopped and took a time-out. Verse 3 says, "God blessed the seventh day and declared it holy, for on it he rested from all his work of creation." It's a pretty good example to follow, don't you think?

Then we hear Jesus saying in Matthew 11:28–29, "Come to me, all of you who are weary and burdened, and I will give you rest. Take up my yoke and learn from me, because I am lowly and humble in heart, and you will find *rest* for your souls" (emphasis added). The word Jesus uses here for "rest" means "to cause to rest, to refresh, to revive, to be calm." Did you know your soul needs rest? Soul rest!

Have you discovered the *rest* Jesus gives? It's available to all who call upon him.

To rest speaks of stopping or ceasing as in Genesis 2. In Matthew 11, to rest speaks of reviving or refreshing or being calm. But what does it mean to rest in God's sovereignty? When the anesthesiologist said, "Enjoy your rest," at that moment I was all in. I was totally, 100 percent in his hands and under his control. I surrendered my rights to him when I signed the release forms and then let him put me to sleep. I was resting in him because I totally trusted them. I didn't fight him, argue with him, or question him. I trusted him. I knew he would take care of me, so I rested. I rested because I trusted him.

Have you discovered that kind of rest? I'm talking about the same kind of rest David expressed in Psalm 62:1: "I am at rest in God alone; my salvation comes from him." And then he had a little talk with his soul in verse 5: "Rest in God alone, my soul, for my hope comes from him." It may be a good day to have a little talk with your soul about this matter of resting in God alone.

Resting in God's sovereignty is trusting him in every circumstance and challenge. It means that you sign the release forms and say, "Lord, you don't have to do one more thing in my life for me to trust you. I know that whatever comes my way comes through you, and it's all to make me more like you and for your glory." That's resting in God's sovereignty. It's saying, "Lord, I know you see things I cannot see and know things I do not know; therefore, I'm in your hands."

Shadrach, Meshach, and Abednego knew about resting in God's sovereignty. In fact, the book of Daniel isn't so much about captives or dreams or prophecies, it's primarily about the sovereignty of God and trusting him. Not far into the book, we hear King Nebuchadnezzar saying in Daniel 4:34, "I, Nebuchadnezzar, looked up to heaven, and my sanity returned to me." Looking up to heaven has a way of altering your sanity! While he saw himself large and God small, he was insane; sanity returned only as he began to see God as all and himself as nothing.[13]

He goes on to say, "Then I praised the Most High and honored and glorified him who lives forever: For his dominion is an everlasting dominion, and his kingdom is from generation to generation" (v. 34). Then he adds in verse 35: "he does what he wants with the army of heaven and the inhabitants of the earth. There is no one who can block his hand or say to him, 'What have you done?'" The king realized there was a greater King than he!

This understanding enabled Shadrach, Meshach, and Abednego to rest in God's sovereignty when their lives were on the line and say in Daniel 3:17–18, "If the God we serve exists, then he can rescue us from the furnace of blazing fire, and he can rescue us from the power of you, the king. But even if he does not rescue us, we want you as king to know that we will not serve your gods or worship the gold statue you set up." That would have been a great place for a mic drop!

The king was so angry he gave orders in verse 19 to "heat the furnace seven times more than was customary." The three were tied up and tossed in the furnace. The next thing we hear the king saying in verse 25 is, "Look! I see four men, not tied, walking around in the fire unharmed; and the fourth looks like a son of the gods."

Don't miss this: those three Hebrews drew strength to rest in God's sovereignty by having a godly companion;

namely—Daniel—not to mention they had one another. We read in Daniel 2:13 about "Daniel and his friends." Again, in verse 17: "Then Daniel went to his house and told his friends." Again, in verse 18: "So Daniel and his friends." The Bible always lists them in the same order, "Daniel and his friends," which tells me that Daniel was their spiritual leader who had poured into their lives.

Do you have godly companions? Do you have any godly influences, perhaps a mentor in your life teaching you about God's sovereignty, teaching you about God's trustworthiness, how you can depend on him in every circumstance? I wonder how well those three men would have fared without Daniel's friendship and influence?

Today's Prayer: *Lord, bring godly people into my life to help me know you better. May I draw strength through their influence to rest in your sovereignty, especially during those times when life doesn't make sense. I know what doesn't make sense to me makes sense to you. In Jesus's name, amen.*

*"If the God we serve exists, then he can rescue
us. . . . But even if he does not rescue us . . ."*
Daniel 3:17–18

Today's Focus: The three Hebrew
children and God's sovereignty.

Today's Insight: Great convictions are essential.

What we believe about God greatly determines how we
respond to life. A. W. Tozer says, "The most portentous
fact about any man is not what he at a given time may say or
do, but what he in his deep heart conceives God to be like.
Were we able to extract from any man a complete answer
to the question, 'What comes to your mind when you think

about God?' we might predict with certainty the spiritual future of that man."[14]

You will never rest in God's sovereignty until you believe God is sovereign. You are a by-product of your God picture. And that internal picture of God determines how you see everything else.[15] Once Nebuchadnezzar saw God in all his sovereignty and strength, how he responded to life changed.

The same thing happened to the prophet Habakkuk. Here's how he responded through the lens of God's sovereignty in Habakkuk 3:17–18: "Though the fig tree does not bud and there is no fruit on the vines, though the olive crop fails and the fields produce no food, though the flocks disappear from the pen and there are no herds in the stalls, yet I will celebrate in the LORD; I will rejoice in the God of my salvation!"

Yes, you read that correctly. How could he celebrate and rejoice with no figs? No fruit? No food? No flocks? He believed in a sovereign God, that's how. What a picture of resting in God's sovereignty. Regardless of your circumstances today, believing God is sovereign can lead you to celebrate and rejoice in the darkest seasons.

After the reality of throat cancer became real to me, believing God is sovereign allowed me to thank him for the cancer. I remember praying, *Lord, though I didn't see this coming, I know you did. I know this didn't catch you by surprise. Knowing you are sovereign and that nothing can get to me without first coming through you, thank you for this cancer. Now use it for your glory and my good.* He did, and he continues using it today for his glory and for my good.

As Shadrach, Meshach, and Abednego faced the furnace, you might wonder how they could so easily surrender to God's sovereignty. Here's how: they had conviction. Their convictions got them into trouble, and their convictions got them through the trouble, not around it.

This whole episode with these three was a setup. According to Daniel 3:8, some of the Chaldeans serving King Nebuchadnezzar had had all they wanted of Shadrach, Meshach, and Abednego, so they began a campaign to get rid of them. They came to the king, reminding him of his decree he issued for everyone to "fall down and worship the gold statue" (v. 10). Then they reminded him of the consequences for failing to bow in verse 11: "Whoever does not fall down and worship will be thrown into a furnace of blazing fire."

Then they brought to his attention in verse 12 that Shadrach, Meshach, and Abednego "have ignored you, the king; they do not serve your gods or worship the gold statue you have set up." The king was furious and had the three rebels brought to him. When he confronted them, he told them in verse 15, "But if you don't worship it, you will immediately be thrown in a furnace of blazing fire—and who is the god who can rescue you from my power?"

You've got to love their response to the king in verse 16: "Nebuchadnezzar, we don't need to give you an answer to this question." Learn this today: the person with great convictions possesses great courage. Convictions are courage producers. They looked at the king and said, "We're not doing it! We're not going along with your godless leadership. We're not compromising. We're not bending or bowing!"

As they faced the furnace, they could quickly surrender to God's sovereignty because they had great convictions. And because they had great convictions, they had great courage. They knew their God; therefore, they trusted their God. It's hard to trust a God you don't know.

Do you know what the great enemy is to convictions? It is compromise. Compromise is like erosion that slowly removes convictions. And once the devil has weakened your convictions, it's just a matter of time before your courage is gone.

How big is your God? The bigger God gets, the smaller our issues will become. Often our problems seem so big because God seems so small. It really boils down to what we believe about God. Over the years, I've been asked, "How do I get more of God in my life?" The answer is simple: you get more of God as God gets more of you. And God gets more of you when you surrender to his sovereignty. There is strength through surrender.

Today's Prayer: *Lord, I do believe in you, and I do believe you. Guide my thinking as I spend time in your Word discovering more about you. May what I believe about you produce ironclad convictions, so that when I'm challenged by the world, I will trust you and not compromise. In Jesus's name, amen.*

DAY 9

"But even if he does not rescue us, . . .
we will not serve your gods."

DANIEL 3:18

Today's Focus: The three Hebrew
children and God's sovereignty.

Today's Insight: Genuine confessions are essential.

Never underestimate the power of a genuine confession. The Bible says in Romans 10:9, "If you confess with your mouth, 'Jesus is Lord,' and believe in your heart that God raised him from the dead, you will be saved." There's a genuine confession that will land you in heaven.

One day Jesus took his disciples on a field trip to Caesarea Philippi and asked them in Matthew 16:13, "Who do people say that the Son of Man is?" and he received several answers. Then he asked his disciples in verse 15, "Who do you say that I am?" Peter responded with a genuine confession in verse 16: "You are the Messiah, the Son of the living God." His confession led to Jesus responding in verse 17, "Blessed are you, Simon son of Jonah."

Shadrach, Meshach, and Abednego were confronted by King Nebuchadnezzar in Daniel 3:14: "Is it true that you don't serve my gods or worship the gold statue I have set up?" Before they could even answer, he continued in verse 15: "Now if you're ready, when you hear the sound of the horn, flute, zither, lyre, harp, drum, and every kind of music, fall down and worship the statue I made. But if you don't worship it, you will immediately be thrown into a furnace of blazing fire—and who is the god who can rescue you from my power?"

For those three it was confession time. They could either deny God and bypass the furnace, or they could surrender to the sovereignty of God and be thrown into the furnace. They learned that day it is better to be in the fire with Jesus than to be out of the fire without him. When confronted with the king's proposal, they didn't need time to huddle up and discuss it. They declared their genuine confession beginning in verse 16: "We don't need to give you an answer to this question. If the God we serve exists, then he can rescue us. . . . But even if he does not rescue us, . . . we will not serve your gods or worship the gold statue you set up." At that moment, we see three men resting in God's sovereignty. It was as if they said,

"We belong to God. We're in his hands, and not even the fires of a furnace can separate us from God."

Their confession landed them in the furnace. Don't let anyone ever tell you that following Jesus gives you a trouble-free life. In fact, the opposite is true. Listen to the warning Jesus gave his followers in John 16:33: "You will have suffering in this world. Be courageous! I have conquered the world." And in Matthew 5:10–12: "Blessed are those who are persecuted because of righteousness, for the kingdom of heaven is theirs. You are blessed when they insult you and persecute you and falsely say every kind of evil against you because of me. Be glad and rejoice, because your reward is great and in heaven. For that is how they persecuted the prophets who were before you."

Let me ask you this: What produced that kind of confession? They were resting in God's sovereignty. As a result, they weren't congratulated; they received no standing ovation; there was no after-church fellowship for the members to meet them and shake their hands. No! We're told in verse 19 that the king "gave orders to heat the furnace seven times more than was customary" (kind of an overkill, don't you think?) and commanded them to be tied up and thrown into "the furnace of blazing fire" (Dan. 3:19–20).

The fire was so hot that it killed the men who carried them to the fire. And then we read in verses 24–25, "Then King Nebuchadnezzar jumped up in alarm. He said to his advisers, 'Didn't we throw three men, bound, into the fire?' 'Yes, of course, Your Majesty,' they replied to the king. He exclaimed, 'Look! I see four men, not tied, walking around in the fire unharmed; and the fourth looks like a son of the gods.'" Now don't miss this. In verse 26 we read that the three Hebrews "came out of the fire." Then verse 27: "the fire had no effect on the bodies of these men: not a hair of their heads was singed, their robes were unaffected, and there was no smell of fire on them."

How many went into the fire? Three. How many did the king see in the fire? Four. How many came out of the fire? Three. Question: Where's the fourth one? He's still in the fire, isn't he? Whenever you find yourself in your next fiery experience, just remember, Jesus is already there waiting for you. Some believe those three Hebrews fulfilled the words of Isaiah 43:1–3, "Do not fear, for I have redeemed you; I have called you by your name; you are mine. When you pass through the waters, I will be with you, and the rivers will not overwhelm you. When you walk through the fire, you will not be scorched, and the flame will not burn you. For I am the LORD your God, the Holy One of Israel, and your Savior."

Do you know what their genuine confession led to? It led to another genuine confession: King Nebuchadnezzar's confession starting in Daniel 3:28: "Praise to the God of Shadrach, Meshach, and Abednego!" His confession continues in verse 29: "Therefore I issue a decree that anyone of any people, nation, or language who says anything offensive against the God of Shadrach, Meshach, and Abednego will be torn limb from limb and his house made a garbage dump. For there is no other god who is able to deliver like this."

We confess for God's glory and our good and for the good of others. One confession led to another confession. Without the confession of the three Hebrews, Nebuchadnezzar never would have made his confession. By resting in God's sovereignty, those three caught the attention of the king, and God changed his heart. Never underestimate the power of your influence by resting in God's sovereignty. Your greatest opportunities to influence others with the gospel are when they observe you resting in God's sovereignty when your world seems out of control.

Today's Prayer: *Give me greater faith that will produce a genuine confession from my lips when my life is coming unraveled. The next time I go through the fire, remind me to look for you. Thank you for waiting for me there. In Jesus's name, amen.*

DAY 10

"My God sent his angel and shut the lions'
mouths; and they haven't harmed me, for I was
found innocent before him. And also before
you, Your Majesty, I have not done harm."
DANIEL 6:22

Today's Focus: Daniel trusting in God's sovereignty.

Today's Insight: Daniel was set apart by his purity.

My wife and I recently flew to Seattle, Washington, to spend a few days with our son and his family. As we approached Seattle, the pilot came on the speaker to inform us that we would be landing in twenty minutes, to turn off our electronic devices, place our trays in their upright position, and adjust our seats. And then he thanked us for flying with them.

Suddenly, those sitting next to the windows started raising their blinds over their windows. What we saw was breathtaking—snowcapped mountains on both sides of the plane—and it was in the month of June! After a few minutes, my wife said to me, "You can tell who's from here and who's not." I said, "Really, how can you tell?" She said, "The ones that aren't from here are all staring out the windows, taking pictures, oohing and aahing, and describing the scenery to the person sitting next to them. But the people that are from here are playing on their iPhones, iPads, watching movies on their laptops, finding a place to stop reading in their books, and not even looking out the windows."

I looked around and she was correct. Those from the area had lost their awe and appreciation of all the beauty around them because they had grown so familiar with it. They had seen it so often it no longer excited and enthused them. They had grown ho-hum with it all. But those of us not so familiar with it were taken aback by its grandeur and beauty like someone whose eyesight had been restored.

Then it dawned on me: familiarity breeds complacency if you let it. You can be around something so long and so often that you stop seeing it. What once excited you now can barely get your attention. Let's face it, it's easy to lose your awe, including of the sovereignty of God. God forbid we reach the point of complacency with his sovereignty.

Those that lose their awe lose their focus. Sometimes it takes a fiery furnace or a den full of hungry lions to snap you out of it. It's hard to lose your awe of God's sovereignty when you're trusting it daily. Daniel was a man like that. Trusting in God's sovereignty was a daily decision for him. He never lost his awe. What set him apart and led him to trust in God's sovereignty is what sets us apart today to trust in his sovereignty: purity.

Yes, Daniel was a man of purity. We don't talk much today about moral purity. It seems to put us at odds with our coworkers, our neighbors, or our classmates, perhaps even with those living under our own roofs. What we learn from Daniel is that it's impossible to rest in God's sovereignty without trusting in God's sovereignty, and it's impossible to trust in God's sovereignty without living a pure life. Not a perfect life, but striving to live a pure life.

When King Darius began his search for men to place in leadership positions in Daniel 6, he included Daniel the Hebrew. We read in verse 3: "Daniel distinguished himself above the administrators and satraps because he had an extraordinary spirit, so the king planned to set him over the whole realm." In other words, he was upbeat, a true optimist. He was the kind of man who always brought a camera with him when he went fishing. He was like that eighty-year-old man who recently got married and bought a four-bedroom house near an elementary school. I'd call that overly optimistic, wouldn't you?

Daniel's "extraordinary spirit" may have landed him a job, but it would eventually land him in a lion's den.

The conspirators immediately went to work. His integrity unified his enemies, and they went together to the king to bring Daniel down. Verse 4 tells us they "kept trying to find a charge against Daniel regarding the kingdom. But they could find no charge or corruption, for he was trustworthy, and no negligence or corruption was found in him." King Nebuchadnezzar said of Daniel that "a spirit of the holy gods is in him" (4:8).

They could find no skeleton in his closet, no smoking gun, no mishandling of money, no inappropriate relationship. This guy was squeaky clean, but that didn't stop them. "Then these men said, 'We will never find any charge against this Daniel unless we find something against him concerning the law of his God'" (6:5). Just like the devil, they paused their efforts only to change their attack plan.

What do you suppose led Daniel to live such a pure life? You say, "It was easier back then to live morally clean. They had no Internet, no iPhones, no iPads. Who couldn't live morally clean?" Really? Well, apparently most of them couldn't. They may not have had the Internet and social media like we do today, but they had to deal with the same thing we have to deal with today: a wicked heart. We're told in Jeremiah 17:9: "The heart is more deceitful than anything else, and incurable—who can understand it?"

That's why we need a new heart. God tells us in Ezekiel 36:26–27, "I will give you a new heart and put a new spirit within you; I will remove your heart of stone and give you a heart of flesh. I will place my Spirit within you and cause you to follow my statues and carefully observe my ordinances."

As I read the Bible, I don't find any new sins being committed today. It wasn't easy to live a morally pure life in Daniel's day just as it's not easy in our day.

What made Daniel an exception to the rule? With corruption and immorality all around him, what kept him motivated and inspired and determined to live above the fray? The same thing that motivates and inspires us today: trusting in and acknowledging God's sovereignty. It's true. What you believe about God determines how you live your life. When you believe God is sovereign, you will want to trust him in every circumstance. When you trust him in every circumstance, you will desire to live morally pure.

Let's end today with this great reminder: it doesn't matter whom you please if you displease God, and it doesn't matter whom you displease if you please God.

Today's Prayer: *Lord, I need a new heart. Come into my life and forgive me of my sin. I'm willing to turn from my sin and turn to you as my Savior and Lord. Help me trust your sovereignty as I trust you as my Savior. In Jesus's name, amen.*

*Three times a day he got down on his
knees, prayed, and gave thanks to his
God, just as he had done before.*

DANIEL 6:10

Today's Focus: Daniel trusting in God's sovereignty.

Today's Insight: Daniel was set apart by his prayers.

Do you have any routines? A routine is a behavior frequently repeated. I've got lots of them! What about you? Do you have any early morning routines? My first morning routine is spending time with God with two cups of coffee. My wife's discovered over the years that it's better not to speak to me until after my second cup of coffee. It's not unusual for us just to wave at each other in the morning's pre-coffee.

What about any evening routines? I have a few bedtime rituals, so much so that my wife will sarcastically ask, "Isn't it about time to begin your routine?" I like to think of it as being disciplined. Most of us have developed some routines, good or bad, over the years and find ourselves in routine ruts. Before you get down on yourself, not all ruts are bad, especially when it comes to our routines. Many routines are good; they keep us focused, grounded, and productive. Most of us function better when following the routines we've developed over the years.

Daniel was a man whose routine had become a rut, a righteous rut. You might ask, "What is a righteous rut?" It's the opposite of an unrighteous rut. You know what that is, don't you? It's those ruts that lead us away from God, and a lot of people today are in them looking for the way out. But a righteous rut is a rut that helps lead you toward God. Those ruts are God's gifts to us, like salvation, by his grace.

Here are a few examples of "righteous ruts" that lead us toward God: a daily time in God's Word is a righteous rut. Corporate and private worship are righteous ruts. Praying is a righteous rut. All three of these disciplines lead us toward God to strengthen our faith and develop our trust in God like that of Daniel. We read in Daniel 6:23: "When Daniel was brought up from the den, he was found to be unharmed, for he trusted in his God."

What landed Daniel in the lions' den? The same thing that landed the lions in the den: a trap. The local administrators and satraps (the local officials) tried to dig up dirt on the outsider Daniel. They found nothing, but they were not quitters. They changed game plans. We read in Daniel 6:7 that they teamed up with other officials and "agreed that the king should establish an ordinance and enforce an edict that, for thirty days, anyone who petitions any god or man except you, the king, will be thrown into the lions' den." When the king agreed, signing it made it "irrevocable" and it "[could not] be changed" (v. 8). Verse 9 says, "So King Darius signed the written edict." The trap was set.

If you were told it was illegal to pray for thirty days, would that change your prayer life? Would your prayer routine come to a screeching halt? How do you think Daniel responded? Do you think he shut down his prayer life and decided to put it on hold until after the king's edict? Do you think he hid in the basement so as not to be caught while praying? Do you think he decided to please man rather than God and take a thirty-day time-out and stop praying? No. No. And no!

So, how did Daniel respond to the king's edict? We're told in verse 10: "When Daniel learned that the document had been signed, he went into his house. The windows in its upstairs room opened toward Jerusalem, and three times a day he got down on his knees, prayed, and gave thanks to his God, just as he done before."

There is a higher law than the law of the land, and that is the law of God. When the law of the land contradicts the law of God, we're to go with God, or as we read in Acts 5:29: "We must obey God rather than people." Daniel's trust in God's sovereignty gave him the courage to obey God rather than man, regardless of the consequences.

Daniel didn't suddenly fall into the righteous rut of praying when faced with opposition. This was no panic prayer, no help-me-out-of-this-mess prayer. He didn't have to introduce himself to God that day. He already knew him. Daniel had been in that righteous prayer rut for years, and as David said in Psalm 55:16–17 (NKJV), "As for me, I will call upon God, and the LORD shall save me. Evening and morning and at noon I will pray, and cry aloud."

Prayer is the rut that helps prepare you for battles, and Daniel had been preparing for years. We find Daniel praying in chapter 2 when he was a younger man, and he's still praying in chapter 6 when he's older. Take another look at verse 10: "just as he had done before." The New King James Version says, "as was his custom since early days." That is, he had been praying from that window three times a day for years. His righteous rut or routine of prayer had strengthened his faith for years, preparing him for this moment.

Now look at what happens in verse 11: "Then these men [the conspirators] went as a group and found Daniel petitioning and imploring his God." Daniel was caught praying. When was the last time your spouse or children or work associate caught you praying? When was the last time you prayed? Daniel's praying set him apart from others and taught him to trust in God's sovereignty. Those who struggle with trusting God's sovereignty during a crisis or challenge are those who have yet to climb into the righteous rut of prayer.

Let's wrap up today's devotional with a sign I read about hanging in a house. It said: "When you're faced with a busy day, save precious time by skipping your devotions. Signed, Satan."

Today's Prayer: *Lord, forgive me for my prayerlessness. Please deepen my desire to talk with you each day. I want to know you more. I want to love you more. I want to trust you more. Give me the courage to stand for what's according to your Word. And this day, I trust your sovereign will and ways for my life. In Jesus's name, amen.*

DAY 12

My God sent his angel and shut the lions'
mouths; and they haven't harmed me,
for I was found innocent before him.

DANIEL 6:22

Today's Focus: Daniel trusting in God's sovereignty.

Today's Insight: Daniel was set apart by his protection.

I often begin my day in the books of Psalms and Proverbs. The psalms teach us about worship, and the proverbs teach us about wisdom. We need both. Today we read Psalm 118:24: "This is the day the LORD has made; let's rejoice and be glad in it." Before your finish your first cup of coffee, it's good to remember that God has made this day and we should rejoice and be glad in it.

You say, "Ernest, how can I rejoice and be glad in it, knowing what I'm facing today?" Remember this regarding today: since God made it, with him you can make it! Not just make it through, but rejoicing and being glad in it. You say, "Even with my health issues today?" Yes. "Even with my financial issues today?" Of course. "Even with my relationship issues today?" Certainly.

You may ask, "How can I rejoice and be glad in this day with all the battles I'm facing?" The same way Daniel faced the lions' den: by resting in God's sovereignty. The psalmist declares in Psalm 103:19: "The LORD has established his throne in heaven, and his kingdom rules over all." Including this day! God made this day for you and me. And in it there is life to live and lessons to learn; therefore, "rejoice and be glad in it" (Ps. 118:24).

In the ups, "rejoice and be glad in it." In the lows, "rejoice and be glad in it" because through them all, God is using both the ups and the downs to conform "to the image of his Son" (Rom. 8:29). Here's another way of saying it: God is using both the ups and downs of today to make you more like Jesus. That's what Romans 8:28 is all about: "We know that all things work together for the good of those who love God, who are called according to his purpose."

Does that include facing hungry lions? How do you think Daniel would answer that question? He may have answered it with a quote from Joseph in Genesis 50:20: "You planned evil against me; God planned it for good." Do you know what Daniel and Joseph and scores of other faithful people down through the ages discovered? They discovered divine protection while resting in God's sovereignty. Learn this today: God's protection seems to follow those who trust him.

We read in Daniel 6:19–20 after a restless night, "At the first light of dawn the king got up and hurried to the lions' den. When he reached the den, he cried out in anguish to Daniel. 'Daniel, servant of the living God,' the king said, 'has your God, whom you continually serve, been able to rescue you from the lions?'" To his surprise, verse 21 says, "Then Daniel spoke." How was it possible? He had spent the night in the lions' den with hungry lions. The last thing the king anticipated that morning was hearing Daniel speaking.

I wonder what was going through Daniel's mind as he responded to the king in verse 21: "May the king live forever." He had waited all night to say those words to the king and to testify of God's protection in verse 22: "My God sent his angel and shut the lions' mouths; and they haven't harmed me, for I was found innocent before him. And also before you, Your Majesty, I have not done harm." And I love verse 23: "When Daniel was brought up from the den, he was found to be unharmed, for he trusted in his God."

Perhaps as Daniel was lowered down into that den, he prayed with the psalmist in Psalm 64:1, "God, hear my voice. . . . Protect my life from the terror of the enemy [lions]." Or Psalm 143:9: "Rescue me from my enemies, LORD; I come to you for protection." And then, coming out of the den the next morning, I can hear him praying with the psalmist again in Psalm 94:22, "But the LORD is my refuge; my God is the rock of my protection." And perhaps during the night, the Lord said as he did in Psalm 91:14–16, "Because he has his heart set on me, I will deliver him; I will protect him because he knows my name. When he calls out to me, I will answer him; I will be with him in trouble. I will rescue him and give him honor. I will satisfy him with a long life and show him my salvation."

God knew where Daniel was, and he knows where you are. He is with you. We read in 2 Chronicles 16:9: "For the eyes of the LORD roam throughout the earth to show himself strong for those who are wholeheartedly devoted to him."

When you find yourself in trouble, where do you look for protection? As the eyes of God roam today across your community looking to "show himself strong," will they fall on you? Are you one on whom God's protection will fall today? Remember this: his protection falls upon "those who are wholeheartedly devoted to him," or as we read in Daniel 6:23: "When Daniel was brought up from the den, he was found unharmed, for he trusted in his God." Read those words again: "those who are wholeheartedly devoted to him" and "for he trusted in his God."

Are you trusting in God's sovereignty today? Are you resting in God's sovereignty today? Are you wholeheartedly devoted to him? If not, why not? If not, why not decide now to put your faith and trust in him?

Let's conclude today where we began with another psalm. One of my favorites is Psalm 3:3–4: "But you, LORD, are a shield around me, my glory, and the one who lifts up my head. I cry aloud to the LORD, and he answers me." There is no better protection than when the Lord is a shield around you. And when he's your shield, he will lift your head in every circumstance. Do you know why he lifts our heads? So we can see and know it is him who is protecting us. So, if you need a head lift today, invite him to be your Savior and shield around you. He will put a song in your heart and a spring in your step.

Today's Prayer: *Lord, thank you that I can trust you today and rest in your sovereignty. I am grateful for the protection you provide me today. Knowing you are my shield, I can walk in faith without fear. I say with the psalmist today in Psalm 119:114, "You are my shelter and my shield; I put my hope in your word." In Jesus's name, amen.*

DAY 13

"I am a woman with a broken heart."

1 SAMUEL 1:15

Today's Focus: Hannah praying within God's sovereignty.

Today's Insight: Looking around, Hannah
contemplated God's sovereignty.

Where can a broken heart find healing? That's what
Hannah wondered as she contemplated the sovereignty
of God. All she wanted was to have a child, a male child, to be
specific. She had a sympathetic, loving husband, but the problem was, he had another wife named Peninnah who didn't care
for Hannah. The institution of polygamy was tolerated under
the law in that day, but it often resulted in sorrow and sin.

71

To make matters worse, Peninnah had conceived and given birth to "sons and daughters" (1 Sam. 1:4). Perhaps Hannah was his first wife, the love of his life. When he later discovered she couldn't bear children, he decided to make Peninnah his wife as well.

The Bible tells us that when their husband, Elkanah, offered sacrifices, "he always gave portions of the meat to his wife Peninnah and to each of her sons and daughters. But he gave a double portion to Hannah, for he loved her even though the LORD had kept her from conceiving" (vv. 4–5).

I can see Hannah looking out the kitchen window, watching her husband playing with his sons while Peninnah was playing games with their girls. Peninnah glances back toward the house, making sure Hannah was watching, while giving her a wicked smile. We're told in verse 6: "Her rival would taunt her severely just to provoke her, because the LORD had kept Hannah from conceiving." To *taunt* speaks of ridiculing or to banter, to anger, to irritate, or provoke.

Peninnah's taunting wasn't a one-time thing. This went on for years. Verse 7 says, "Year after year, when she went up to the LORD's house, her rival taunted her in this way." Year after year! Peninnah wouldn't let up. Perhaps because she knew that Hannah was the love of Elkanah's life and that she could never capture his heart. So Peninnah, like Satan, attacked Hannah at her weakest point: her barrenness.

In that day, a woman's self-worth was tied to her ability to give her husband children. And not being able to meant that she was a failure and a disappointment to him and herself. No wonder we read in verse 10 that she was "deeply hurt" and "wept with many tears" and in verse 15: "I am a woman with a broken heart."

What is missing from your life causing you to feel unfulfilled and unsatisfied? Perhaps like Hannah, you're contemplating the sovereignty of God, wondering why God isn't doing something. You may feel like your life is stuck in neutral, keeping you from moving forward. But nothing could be further from the truth. Neutral is when God is either working in you or arranging circumstances so he can work in you. Either way, God is always working to make things happen.

Do you know why an automobile has a neutral setting? Without neutral, your car cannot move from one gear to the next. It must have a neutral to move you forward and backyard. Neutral has a purpose. God is never in neutral. He is always working to fulfill his plans and purposes in us and through us and around us for his glory and our good and for the good of others. Hannah discovered that reality as she contemplated the sovereignty of God.

Perhaps today, like Hannah, you, too, have a broken heart. Someone or something has deeply hurt you by words or actions. Sometimes broken hearts and deep hurts come from what we perceive as God withholding something good from us. That is what broke Hannah's heart. She lived to bear children. God created her to bear children. God placed in her heart a mothering instinct. Since early childhood, she probably spent her days dreaming of the day when she would have her own children to nurture and care for.

Then came the day she married Elkanah. God brought him into her life to care for and to protect and to love her and to give her children. After all, that was her dream since childhood. But children didn't come. She never had a positive pregnancy test. Her opportunity to bear children was fading away like fog on a sunny day, leaving her broken and deeply hurt.

Have your unfulfilled dreams left you brokenhearted? Today you may be contemplating the sovereignty of God as you look around, seeing how God has given others what you have dreamed of having yourself and asking, "Why him? Why her? Why them? What do they have that I don't have? Why not me? After all, I love God and serve God. Why is God withholding his goodness and blessing from me?"

May I give you some good news? God specializes in healing broken hearts and mending deep hurts. Listen to his words to Moses in Exodus 15:26: "I am the LORD who heals you." This word *heals* has several shades of meaning. It means to mend, as a garment is mended; to repair, as a building is reconstructed; to cure, as a diseased person is restored to health.[16] To mend. To repair. To cure. This same word is found in Jeremiah 30:17: "But I will bring you health and will heal you of your wounds—this is the LORD's declaration."

Brokenhearted today? God is near. Psalm 34:18 says, "The LORD is near the brokenhearted; he saves those crushed in spirit."

Do you have any wounds that need to be healed? God is a healer. Psalm 147:3, "He heals the brokenhearted and bandages their wounds."

In 1 Samuel 1:15 we read that Hannah was brokenhearted. Then Hannah's heart was rejoicing (2:1). And in between her broken heart and rejoicing heart was the sovereignty of God at work. God can replace a broken heart with a rejoicing one. Within his sovereignty there is healing. He heals what no person can heal.

Today's Prayer: *Lord, as I contemplate your sovereignty and what it means in my life, I have many questions, just as Hannah did. And like Hannah, I have a broken heart that needs to be healed and deep wounds that need mending. Help me trust you are working to fulfill my unmet needs. May you replace my broken heart with a rejoicing heart. In Jesus's name, amen.*

DAY 14

"I've been pouring out my heart before the LORD."

1 SAMUEL 1:15

Today's Focus: Hannah praying within God's sovereignty.

Today's Insight: Looking within, Hannah counted on God's sovereignty.

How is your prayer life? When was the last time you prayed to God? We often treat prayer as a last resort when everything else has failed. After we have exhausted our resources, tried everything we know to try, we then try prayer.

Hannah, like all of us, had an unmet, unfulfilled need in her life. For her it was being barren. What is your unmet need, and how are you seeking to have it met? I believe Hannah had reached the end of her rope. Have you ever been there? After years of trying to have a child and after years of facing the ridicule of Peninnah and after shedding enough tears to fill the ocean, Hannah took action. We read in 1 Samuel 1:9: "On one occasion . . ."

How many occasions had she experienced? A lot. I cannot tell you the exact number, but there were many of them. Verse 7 tells us: "Year after year, when she went up to the LORD's house, her rival taunted her in this way." Don't miss this! Hannah wasted *years* of unnecessary grief and guilt trying to resolve her own unmet need. The tragedy is that many of us do the same thing today. Rather than living in victory, we live in defeat. Rather than living fulfilled, we live unfulfilled. Rather than counting on God's sovereignty, we count on our own strength, leaving us like Hannah, "deeply hurt," weeping "with many tears," and with "a broken heart" (vv. 10, 15).

Enough is enough! In fact, God is enough. He's always enough. He's more than enough. God wants you to discover what Abraham discovered in Genesis 22:14: "The LORD Will Provide." Do you know what makes that possible? His sovereignty. We read in Psalm 103:19: "The LORD has established his throne in heaven, and his kingdom rules over all." Here's another insightful passage from Psalm 48:14: "This God, our God forever and ever—he will always lead us." It's time to begin counting on God's sovereignty rather than your own strength and wisdom. After years of struggling, Hannah reached the end of her rope. She was exhausted, deeply hurt, and brokenhearted, but she finally let go and decided to count on God's sovereignty.

Notice in 1 Samuel 1:10 *her prayer to God*: "Deeply hurt, Hannah prayed to the LORD and wept with many tears." Hannah took her unmet need, and she talked to God about it. Do you think having an unmet need increased or decreased her prayer life? It increased it! Without her unmet need, her prayer life would not have been as intense. She had prayed before, but her prayer life went to another level because of her unmet need. Some of the greatest periods of prayer throughout my life have been the result of unmet needs. I once heard someone say, "Anything that drives you to God is a good thing."

If you have a secret grief, an unmet need that brings you dissatisfaction or unfulfillment, learn where to take it. Learn from Hannah. She took it to the Lord in prayer. If someone asked Hannah what she had learned from this time in her life, I can hear her say, "I would have brought my unmet needs to the Lord sooner rather than wasting those years being unnecessarily hurt and brokenhearted."

Notice *her plea to God* in verse 11: "Making a vow, she pleaded, 'LORD of Armies, if you will take notice of your servant's affliction, remember and not forget me, and give your servant a son. . . .'" She prayed specifically, not generally. Rather than asking God for a child, she specifically asked for a son.

Do you pray specifically or generally? Specific prayers receive specific answers, and general prayers receive general answers. Listen to what God told Solomon in 1 Kings 3:5: "Ask. What should I give you?" God says in Jeremiah 33:3,

"Call to me and I will answer you and tell you great and incomprehensible things you do not know."

Are your prayers specific? Are you praying specifically about that unmet need that's left you feeling unfulfilled and unsatisfied? Stop beating around the bush with God and *ask him*. Pour out your heart before the Lord like Hannah did in verse 15. Where is your passion? Where are your tears? Hannah said in verse 16, "I've been praying from the depth of my anguish and resentment." Her passion in prayer caused Eli the priest to think she was drunk. In verse 14 he asked her, "How long are you going to be drunk? Get rid of your wine!" We read in James 4:2–3: "You do not have because you do not ask. You ask and don't receive because you ask with wrong motives, so that you may spend it on your pleasures."

Hannah prayed until she received an answer. That's the kind of praying Jesus is talking about in Matthew 7:7–8 when he said, "Ask, and it will be given to you. Seek, and you will find. Knock, and the door will be opened to you. For everyone who asks receives, and the one who seeks finds, and to the one who knocks, the door will be opened."

We should note that all three of the verbs Jesus uses here (*ask*, *seek*, and *knock*) are in the present tense. All three of them speak of continual action. He was literally saying, "Ask and keep on asking. Seek and keep on seeking. Knock and keep on knocking." How long should we ask, seek, and knock? Until God says yes or until God says no or until his Spirit says to our spirit, "Not now."

Has there ever been a time when your prayers were so passionate that someone accused you of drinking wine? Pour out your heart to him. Go ahead. He's waiting for you to come to him in prayer. Be like Hannah, who was one prayer away from having her unfulfilled need met by God. Don't stop praying until you receive an answer.

Today's Prayer: *Lord, forgive my lack of faith and for counting on everything and everyone to meet the unfulfilled need in my life. You're all I have left. It's either you or nothing. I place my need before you, counting on your sovereignty. If you meet my need, I will rejoice. If you don't, I will rejoice. Give me the faith to rest in your sovereignty. In Jesus's name, amen.*

DAY 15

Making a vow, she pleaded, "LORD of Armies,
if you will . . . give your servant a son, I will
give him to the LORD all the days of his life."

1 SAMUEL 1:11

Today's Focus: Hannah praying within God's sovereignty.

Today's Insight: Looking back, Hannah
celebrated God's sovereignty.

If you were asked to name the shortest verse in the Bible, you would probably say John 11:35, "Jesus wept," and you would be wrong! The shortest verse in the Bible is 1 Thessalonians 5:16, "Rejoice always." Now I can already hear you thinking, "How can that be true? It looks like there's a tie for the shortest verse." There's no tie but rather a clear winner.

In John 11:35, the Greek New Testament has three words, which literally say, "The Jesus wept." In 1 Thessalonians 5:16, the Greek text only has two words, which literally say, "Always rejoice," making it the shortest verse in the Bible. One verse speaks of weeping while the shortest verse speaks of rejoicing. We find both weeping and rejoicing in 1 Samuel 1–2 regarding Hannah, wife of Elkanah.

To add to her grief and hurt of not bearing children, every time she traveled to Shiloh with her husband and his other wife for worship, her rival taunted and provoked her. We're told in 1 Samuel 1:7: "Year after year, when she went up to the Lord's house, her rival taunted her in this way." You've got to hand it to Hannah: even though she knew her rival was going to taunt and provoke her every year, she kept going. I've known people to drop out of church for much less.

We saw yesterday her prayer and plea to the Lord. Look what she did in verse 11: "Making a vow, she pleaded." Be careful making vows to God. We read in Psalm 76:11: "Make and keep your vows to the Lord your God." God holds us to our vows. As Hannah's prayer continues in verse 11, out of her sanctified determination, notice *her promise to God*: ". . . if you will give your servant a son, [and] I will give him to the Lord all the days of his life, and his hair will never be cut." Her promise was if he gave her a son, she would give him right back to God for his glory. She was saying, "Lord, if you give me a son, I'll do my part to influence him to grow up to be a man of God." Did she? Yes! God gave her a son. Yes, she kept her promise. We will hear Hannah say in 1 Samuel 1:27–28, "I prayed for this boy, and since the LORD gave me what I asked him for, I now give the boy to the LORD. For as long as he lives, he is given to the LORD."

Perhaps like Hannah, you've tried everything you know to try to have that unmet, unfulfilled need met in your life. When all you have left for help is God, he's ready to step in. Within God's sovereignty, you can know God will meet your need. Within his sovereignty, there is a *yes*, a *no*, or a *not now* waiting for you. Regardless of his answer, you can trust him. Rest in his sovereignty.

After hearing Hannah pray, "from the depth of [her] anguish and resentment" (v. 16), "Eli responded, 'Go in peace, and may the God of Israel grant the request you've made of him.' 'May your servant find favor with you,' she replied. Then Hannah went on her way; she ate and no longer looked despondent" (vv. 17–18).

When she heard Eli's response, her appetite returned, and you've got to love the last words of verse 18: "She ate and no longer looked despondent." She not only had a faith-lift, but she also had a face-lift! God spoke to her through his servant. Her countenance changed in a moment. Her pain was replaced with peace. Her broken heart was replaced with a healed heart. Her weeping would soon be replaced with rejoicing.

Did you notice who went to worship the next morning (v. 19)? "The next morning Elkanah and Hannah got up early to worship before the LORD." Hannah was all in. She wasn't going to miss worship that day! Nobody had to force her to get up early the next day to worship the Lord. Hannah's heart was full of joy and peace and praise. She knew it was only a matter of time before her unfulfilled need was met by God. After worship that day, they packed up and returned home to Ramah. Verse 19 says, "and the LORD remembered her." Then in verse 20 we read:, "After some time, Hannah conceived and gave birth to a son. She named him Samuel, because she said, 'I requested him from the LORD,'" Hannah conceived! I wonder what Peninnah thought when she received the big announcement. I can hear her now: "There is no way! She can't conceive! She needs to get her money back from that pregnancy test." You can believe she was devastated.

After Hannah weaned him, verse 24 says, "she took him with her to Shiloh. . . . Though the boy was still young, she took him to the LORD's house at Shiloh." She did what every God-loving parent would do. She brought her child to church when he "was still young." You can't start bringing them too early, but you can start too late.

Hannah found Eli the priest and said, "I prayed for this boy, and since the LORD gave me what I asked for, I now give the boy to the LORD" (vv. 27–28).

Take a few minutes and carefully read Hannah's prayer in chapter 2. She begins by saying in verse 1, "My heart rejoices in the LORD." Listen as she declares God's sovereignty in verse 7: "The LORD brings poverty and gives wealth; he humbles and he exalts," and in verse 10: "Those who oppose the LORD will be shattered; he will thunder in the heavens against them. The LORD will judge the ends of the earth. He will give power to his king."

Someone asks, "Where does prayer fit within the sovereignty of God? If God is sovereign, is prayer necessary? After all, he does what he wants." Yes, he does what he wants, and he wants us praying like loving parents want to hear from their children.

Today's Prayer: *Lord, today I celebrate your sovereignty over my life. As I seek your will, I surrender to your ways. Looking back over my life, I can see how you've guided my steps, though at times I resisted. May my trust in you grow, enabling me to rest in your sovereignty. In Jesus's name, amen.*

DAY 16

There is no one holy like the LORD.
There is no one besides you! And
there is no rock like our God.

1 SAMUEL 2:2

Today's Focus: Hannah praying within God's sovereignty.

Today's Insight: Looking overall, Hannah
had many takeaways in her life.

H alfway through something is often a pivotal position. If
you don't believe me, ask a college student who is halfway
through their education. The dropout rate has been on the
increase for years. What about the vehicle you're currently
driving? Halfway through paying for it is often when people

decide to purchase a new one, driving themselves into deeper debt. Halfway through can be costly.

How many projects do you have that are halfway completed? Your intentions were good. You planned to complete it within days. But there it sits in your garage or house unfinished, incomplete, and you hear those encouraging words, "When are you going to finish that project?" We've all been there.

I've discovered that it is easier to start a project than to finish one. That reality causes me to think twice before starting any project. You can't finish what you don't start, right?

Reader, I want to congratulate you for pushing through the halfway mark of our thirty-day journey on resting in God's sovereignty. I hope along the way God is giving you a new perspective on his sovereignty and what it means in your life. You may have more questions now about his sovereignty than you had before starting this journey. That's not necessarily bad if you continue to seek the answers.

During the last two weeks, we have discovered that resting in God's sovereignty causes the fire in the pit not to be so hot, the lions in the dens not to be so hungry, and the difficulties of life not to be so hopeless. As my friend often prays, "Lord, I'm glad you're God and I'm not." There is a peace that "surpasses all understanding," as Paul declared (Phil. 4:7), when we've grown to trust God enough to enable us to rest each day in his sovereignty. My prayer for you is that your trust in God is growing so that you can rest in his sovereignty. After all, he's God and you're not!

During the last few days, our focus has been on Hannah. I find myself at times becoming frustrated in writing a devotional book because space on the page is limited to the highlights. Therefore, let's consider a few biblical principles from the life of Hannah that speak to us and how God deals with his children.

First, God specializes in meeting the needs of his children. Eight words Hannah thought she would never hear: "Hannah conceived and gave birth to a son" (1 Sam. 1:20). Can you image her emotion when she discovered she was pregnant? I can hear her crying out to her husband, "I don't believe it! We're going to have a child! God has heard our prayers! He has seen our tears! We're going to have a son, for our God is sovereign."

God often allows a need in our life to meet it. He allows us to get hungry to feed us. He allows us to grow tired to give us rest. He allows us to be lonely to provide us fellowship. The list is limitless. Like Hannah, the next time you have a need in your life, talk to God about it, and then give him time to work.

Second, God gives back more than what we give him. Are you familiar with the principle of sowing and reaping? The Bible speaks of it in 2 Corinthians 9:6: "The person who sows sparingly will also reap sparingly, and the person who sows generously will also reap generously." That passage is primarily talking about giving tithes and offerings, but the principle reaches beyond our money. It impacts our very lives. I've heard on occasion the principle of sowing and reaping explained like this: we reap what we sow, we reap after we sow, and we reap more than we sow.

Hannah experienced this principle firsthand. In keeping her vow to God, she said, "I now give the boy to the LORD. For as long as he lives, he is given to the LORD" (1 Sam. 1:28), just as she promised she would if God gave her a son. He did and she did.

Years later, as her son Samuel was serving God, Hannah and Elkanah went to Shiloh to worship, and in 2:20 we read: "Eli [the priest] would bless Elkanah and his wife: 'May the LORD give you children by this woman in place of the one she has given to the LORD.' Then they would go home." The next verse says: "The LORD paid attention to Hannah's need, and she conceived and gave birth to three sons and two daughters" (v. 21).

She gave one son to God, and God gave her back three sons and two daughters! That's quite a return on her investment! That is how the principle of sowing and reaping works.

Third, God hears the prayers of his children. Did you know God is waiting to hear from you? He is! He tells us in Jeremiah 33:3, "Call to me and I will answer you and tell you great and incomprehensible things you do not know." Jesus says in Matthew 7:7, "Ask, and it will be given to you," and in John 16:23–24, "Truly I tell you, anything you ask the Father in my name, he will give you." And then he says in verse 24, "Ask and you will receive, so that your joy may be complete."

God invites us to ask him! You say, "Ask him what?" Whatever your need is. Whatever your unfulfilled dream is.

Does God always answer? Yes, every time within his sovereignty. Aren't you glad God hasn't answered all your prayers the way you may have wished in the beginning? I am, because I have prayed some selfish, stupid prayers over the years. I have found it is better to pray seeking his will than requesting my wants. He knows what Ernest Easley needs more than Ernest Easley does. And because I know that, as I pray, I can rest in his sovereignty.

Today's Prayer: *Lord, thank you for meeting the needs in my life. No one can meet my needs like you. I know you stand ready to hear from me and help me overcome what comes my way today. Give me a deeper desire to talk to you every day and to keep my hands opened, not clenched. Thank you for being my sovereign Savior. In Jesus's name, amen.*

DAY 17

There was a man in Jerusalem whose name
was Simeon. This man was righteous and
devout, looking forward to Israel's consolation,
and the Holy Spirit was on him.

LUKE 2:25

Today's Focus: Simeon looking for the
fulfillment of God's sovereignty.

Today's Insight: Simeon was spiritually guarded.

If you were asked to name the characters found in the
Christmas account recorded in Luke 2, how many could
you name? I'm confident Mary and Joseph would make the
list, followed by perhaps the shepherds and, of course, an angel
of the Lord. I would hope Jesus would make your list. What

about Caesar Augustus? You need to add him if you haven't already.

We are reintroduced to these people every year around Christmas. Many families read Luke's Christmas account on Christmas Day prior to opening presents or before the big Christmas meal. If that's not part of your Christmas tradition, you may want to consider including it. Something about reading the Christmas account helps keep everyone focused on what Christmas is all about.

Now, back to the Christmas account. There were Mary and Joseph, the angel of the Lord, the shepherds, Caesar Augustus, and, of course, Jesus. But also included in the Christmas account was a man named Simeon. He is often overlooked because he wasn't in Bethlehem where the birth of Jesus took place. Besides, we usually stop reading around verses 13–14 with "Suddenly there was a multitude of the heavenly host with the angel, praising God and saying: Glory to God in the highest heaven, and peace on earth to people he favors!" At about that point during our Christmas services, we light the candles and sing "Silent Night," and then go home. Don't stop at verse 14!

If you keep reading, you'll find that the shepherds then headed to Bethlehem, where they found baby Jesus lying in a manger. Then comes verse 21 that tells us on the eighth day, as according to their law, the Baby (Jesus) would be circumcised. Mary and Joseph got their personal belongings together and headed a short distance to Jerusalem to dedicate Jesus to God at the temple and offer a sacrifice.

That brings us to verses 25–26: "There was a man in Jerusalem whose name was Simeon. This man was righteous and devout, looking forward to Israel's consolation, and the Holy Spirit was on him. It had been revealed to him by the Holy Spirit that he would not see death before he saw the Lord's Messiah."

Don't miss this: "and the Holy Spirit was on him." I wonder how they knew that? What was it about Simeon that caused people to say of him, "and the Holy Spirit was on him"? This man was different and not in a bad way. His demeanor was different. His decisions were different. His direction was different. In fact, the Bible describes him as being "righteous," which means he was an upright, just, and fair person. It speaks of someone who is in right standing with God. Being "righteous" or "just" meant he was right with God.

He was also described as a "devout" person, which means he was a God-fearing man. This word *devout* literally means "to take hold." It speaks of someone who carefully takes what's held out to them. Rather than rejecting God's offer of salvation, he received it. He took it. By receiving it, he became a devout and devoted man of God. He had a healthy, holy fear of God, which led him to make certain choices. Being *righteous* and *devout* are some of those "fruit of righteousness" the writer of Hebrews mentions (12:11).

Simon was righteous and devout because the Holy Spirit was on him. Those attributes are not produced by the flesh but by the Spirit of God. The Greek New Testament says that the Holy Spirit literally "existed or lived" on him. What an incredible thought. The Holy Spirit lived on him. When someone describes you, do they say, "and the Holy Spirit lives on you"? Within God's sovereignty is the Holy Spirit that produces in you the fruit of righteousness and the fear of God.

Let's get back to Simeon. We read an incredible promise God gave him in Luke 2:26: "It had been revealed to him by the Holy Spirit that he would not see death before he saw the Lord's Messiah." The Holy Spirit is not only the fruit producer, but he is also the truth revealer. He reveals God's truth to us. That's why a nonbeliever can read a Bible verse and then walk away scratching his head, wondering what it meant, and a believer can read the same verse and walk away rejoicing in his heart at what it means. One has the Holy Spirit revealing God's truth while the other one doesn't.

Learn this today: the Holy Spirit reveals God's truth to those he lives in. That's why you'll never understand the Bible without the presence of the Holy Spirit in your life. That's what Jesus was talking about in John 14:26: "But the Counselor, the Holy Spirit, whom the Father will send in my name, will teach you all things and remind you of everything I have told you."

He is the teacher! He is the revealer! He is the reminder!

What did the Holy Spirit reveal to Simeon? "[H]e would not see death before he saw the Lord's Messiah" (Luke 2:26). God supernaturally revealed to Simeon that he wouldn't die before Christmas, that he wouldn't see death until he saw the Savior. Do you know what that made Simeon? He was a spiritually guarded man. No bullet could take him out. No knife could take him out. No sickness could take him out. He couldn't be run over by a camel trying to cross the street until "he saw the Lord's Messiah."

In a way, he was immortal until he saw the Lord's Messiah. That's what the Holy Spirit revealed to him. Afterward, I wonder if it changed how Simeon lived? I wonder if he stopped looking both ways before crossing a street. You know what I mean? Or was he the same old Simeon living out his days waiting for the day he would see the Messiah? He lived each day, guarded by the Holy Spirit, with the anticipation of the Messiah's birth. I can see him waking up every morning and asking himself, *Is this the day? Will my eyes behold the long-awaited Messiah? Is this Christmas Day?*

Had it been me, I would have woken up every morning with mixed feelings thinking, *If I don't see him today, my life on earth isn't over. If I see him today, my life on earth is over.*

In one sense, what was true for Simeon is true for us. We, too, are here on this earth until our work on earth is done. That means nothing can take us from here until our work is done, and nothing can keep us here after our work is done. The sovereignty of God is what makes that possible.

Today's Prayer: *Lord, I am grateful that within your sovereignty I am safe to serve you today. Forgive me of all my sin, and fill me with your Holy Spirit. May those around me see that your Spirit is on me. I anticipate your Spirit producing in me the fruit of righteousness so that my life may be maximized for you. In Jesus's name, amen.*

DAY 18

Guided by the Spirit, he entered the temple.

LUKE 2:27

Today's Focus: Simeon looking for the
fulfillment of God's sovereignty.

Today's Insight: Simeon was spiritually guided.

I have been leading groups to Israel for many years. I've found that traveling to Israel will enlighten the Word of God, enhance your worship of him, and energize your walk with him if you have a relationship with him through his Son, Jesus Christ.

What makes or breaks a trip to Israel is the guide. I've had some good guides over the years and some bad ones. On one trip, our group was in the hotel lobby about to load the bus, and we couldn't find the guide. I called his room with no answer. I called his cell number, again no answer. Then I went to the front desk to see if they could find him. A man at the front desk told me he would go to his room to check on him. When he found him, he was fast asleep!

What is worse than a bad guide is no guide. As many times as I've been, I can't imagine traveling across Israel with no guide at all, and here's why:

- A guide knows more than I know.
- A guide knows how to get places I don't know.
- A guide knows where the best restaurants are located.
- A guide knows where the dangerous places are located.
- A guide knows where the bathrooms are.

The older I get, the more important that last one has become! The bottom line is that guides know more than I know. Their job is to get me places on time, explain the history of each site, and keep me safe.

Do you know what we need more than a guide for Israel? We need a guide for life. Someone who knows more than we know. Someone to get us places we don't know anything about. Someone to help us avoid dangerous places. Someone we can depend on not to sleep in when we're heading out. Simeon had a guide like that. We read about him in Luke 2:27: "Guided by the Spirit, he entered the temple."

Did you know that when you trust Jesus Christ as your Lord and Savior and invite him into your life, you become indwelled by the Holy Spirit? He indwells you to guide you just as he did with Simeon. Like with Simeon, He guides our thoughts, our decisions, and our steps. He even guides the timing of our steps to make sure we're in the right place at the right time to fulfill the purposes and plans of God. In fact, included in Zechariah's prophecy we read in Luke 1:79, "guide our feet into the way of peace."

When did the Holy Spirit guide Simeon to enter the temple? The very moment Jesus's parents brought him to the temple to be circumcised. God specializes in arranging divine appointments within his sovereignty. The Holy Spirit guided Mary and Joseph to bring Jesus to the temple that day at the same time he guided Simeon to go to the temple. Why? To fulfill the promise of God "that he [Simeon] would not see death before the saw the Lord's Messiah" (Luke 2:26). In the temple that day, the sovereignty of God was in full stride.

Is the Holy Spirit guiding you these days? His guidance begins when you receive the Holy Spirit through salvation. Then comes a daily filling of the Holy Spirit as we confess and repent of our sin. He cannot fill what isn't empty. He cannot guide what he doesn't fill. Are you being filled with him daily? Today's question is: Are you a Spirit-filled follower of Jesus? I'm talking about a filling that takes place every day. You say, "Ernest, why every day?" Because we leak every day! With every sin, we leak. That means every day we need a filling for him to "guide [us] into all the truth," as Jesus mentions in John 16:13.

Our desire should be to say along with David in Psalm 16:8, "I always let the LORD guide me. Because he is at my right hand, I will not be shaken." You may be asking, "How does the Holy Spirit guide or lead us today?" Let's focus on three psalms to help us know how we can be guided by the Spirit like Simeon.

First, there is Psalm 25:5: "Guide me in your truth and teach me, for you are the God of my salvation." The Spirit of God guides us as we spend time in God's Word. Don't neglect your time each day in God's Word. If you want the Spirit of God to lead you, then feed on his Word. Where there is no feeding, there's no leading.

Second, there is Psalm 26:3: "For your faithful love guides me, and I live by your truth." God also guides us by his faithful love. How does he do that? The same way loving parents guide their children. Because God loves us and is faithful, we can always depend on him to guide us:

- to help us, never to harm us.
- toward holiness, never away from holiness.
- in his direction, never away from his direction.
- to be more like Jesus, never more like the world.
- in the direction of selflessness, never in the direction of selfishness.

Third, there is Psalm 73:24: "You guide me with your counsel." God always guides us to live by his Word. In high school we had a guidance counselor. He was older than I. He had more experience and knew more than I. He had already been where I was in life. His responsibility was to help guide me in what courses to take, which teachers were best, how to prepare for college, etc.

We have someone better than a guidance counselor; we have the Holy Spirit to guide and lead us through all the dangers we face. Charles Spurgeon reminds us that "the swallow flies across the ocean by instinct. Animals migrate. Ants store food by instinct. Man has none. He has no foresight. He cannot see far before him. He never went this way before."[17]

Just as the Holy Spirit guided Simeon, he guides us today. He guides us by his love. He guides us by his truth. He guides us by his council. Hallelujah! What a Savior.

Today's Prayer: *Lord, thank you for the presence of your Holy Spirit. As I confess my sins to you today, I empty myself of sin. I now ask you to fill my emptiness with your Holy Spirit, to guide and lead my steps as you did with Simeon. Thank you that I can rest in your sovereignty as I depend on your guidance. In Jesus's name, amen.*

DAY 19

Simeon took him up in his arms, praised God,
and said, "Now, Master, you can dismiss
your servant in peace, as you promised."
LUKE 2:28–29

Today's Focus: Simeon looking for the
fulfillment of God's sovereignty.

Today's Insight: Simeon was spiritually grateful.

I have conducted hundreds of funerals over the years, including several for family members. When you are the pastor, the family expects you to say something kind about their loved one. After all, it's their funeral! But truthfully, there have been times when I struggled with giving a positive eulogy.

It reminds me of a story about a pastor who was approached by a family to conduct the funeral of their loved one. Everyone knew the man who had died to be a cheat, a drunk, and a womanizer. As the pastor visited with the man's brother, whose reputation was worse than his deceased brother, he requested him to say in his eulogy that his brother was a saint. The pastor knew he couldn't say that because everyone in the community knew the man's character. So the pastor told the family he couldn't do the funeral. The brother of the deceased was disappointed and then told the pastor he was going to pay him $5,000 for conducting the service.

The next day as the pastor stood to give the eulogy, he began by telling when and where the man was born, the names of his family members, those who had preceded him in death, what he did for a living, and his accomplishments in life. He then said, "And compared to his brother, he was a saint."

Hopefully, when it comes time for someone to give your eulogy, they won't have to struggle and stretch the truth. In Luke 2, we find this man named Simeon eulogizing, not from a broken heart but from a joyful heart, not from a grief-filled heart but from a grateful heart. He wasn't eulogizing the dead but the living. His eulogies revealed he was spiritually grateful. You ask, "Grateful for what?" Grateful for the sovereignty of God. If there was ever a man who rested in God's sovereignty, it was Simeon.

The Holy Spirit had made known to him "that he would not see death before he saw the Lord's Messiah" (Luke 2:26), which is another way of saying he wasn't going to experience death until after Jesus's birth. The Holy Spirit spoke to him, saying, "Simeon, stop what you're doing and go immediately to the temple." Simeon, whose name means "one who hears and obeys," headed to the temple. When he arrived, sure enough, Mary and Joseph had just arrived there with the Lord's Messiah, we read in verse 27, "to perform for him what was customary under the law."

Can you guess what happened next? Verse 28 says, "Simeon took him up in his arms." If you're a parent, you probably remember the first time you held your child. For most of us, it was an unexplainable emotional moment of joy unmatched by any other event. There were tears of joy that your long-awaited child had finally arrived.

Can you imagine the emotions of Simeon, as he held in his arms the long-awaited Messiah and saw the Lord's salvation? His heart was full of joy. His joy tank was filled to the brim! With a full tank of joy, we read of *Simeon's praise*. Verse 28 tells us that he "praised God." The Greek word translated "praised" is where we get the word *eulogy*. Simeon eulogized God! You ask, "How do you eulogize God?" By speaking well of him, that's how. In fact, the word *eulogy* means "to bless, praise, or to speak well of." Simeon blessed God. Simeon praised God. Simeon spoke well of God. Wouldn't you like to know what he included in his eulogy?

What do you include when you speak well of God? Do you include gratitude for what he's done and is doing in your life? Do you tell others the difference he's made in your life? How about including his mercy and grace and patience and persistence? What else do you include when you eulogize or speak well of God? What should you include?

With the Christ child in his arms, rejoicing at the fulfillment of God's sovereignty in his life and being spiritually grateful, he praised God! Simeon's time of praising was followed by *his prayer* in verses 29–32. Take a moment to carefully read through it. He prays in verse 29, "You can dismiss your servant in peace, as you promised." In other words, "Now I'm ready to die."

Are you ready to die? No one is truly ready to live or die until they take hold of Jesus. It's been said that you are not ready to live until you are ready to die. Once your eternal destiny is settled through a relationship with Jesus Christ, you no longer fear death the way you once did because you are ready. That's how Simeon could pray, "You can dismiss your servant in peace." It's possible to live and die in peace.

His prayer continues in verse 30, "For my eyes have seen your salvation." He didn't refer to Jesus as the way of salvation or the worker of salvation but salvation itself. He had in his arms the salvation of God, the same salvation of God we now have in our hearts.

After his prayer we read of *Simeon's prophecy*, starting in verse 33, as he blesses or eulogizes Mary and Joseph. In his brief prophecy, Simeon speaks of the coming *opposition* in verse 34: "Indeed, this child is destined to cause the fall and rise of many in Israel and to be a sign that will be opposed." That's what every parent wants to hear about their child, right? Then he mentions the coming *affliction* in verse 35: "and a sword will pierce your own soul." And then finally he mentions the *coming revelation*: "that the thoughts of many hearts may be revealed." That is, this child will reveal the condition of many hearts toward the things of God. What's on the inside of a person will be revealed on the outside. Jesus is still revealing the conditions of hearts today. What is he revealing about yours? Is he revealing an open heart to his Word or a closed heart? Is he revealing a hot heart or a cold heart toward the things of God? Is he revealing a pliable heart or a hard heart toward the things of God? Jesus is the great revealer.

God kept his promise to Simeon. He wouldn't die until he had seen the Lord's Messiah. I find it interesting that there is no record of Simeon's death. We know he died, but there is no record of it. I wonder how many days or months or perhaps years Simeon lived after he saw the Lord's Messiah. However long it was, you can know he spent it eulogizing or speaking well of Jesus. Eulogies are not only for the dead but also for the living. However long you have left on earth, speak well of Jesus. Speak well of Jesus today. One good word to a struggling soul could forever change their eternal destiny.

Today's Prayer: *Lord, thank you for being a promise maker and promise keeper. Bring someone across my path today who needs to hear a good word about Jesus. May I be quick to eulogize my living Savior to the spiritually dead. May they receive him and experience spiritual life. In Jesus's name, amen.*

She was well along in years, having lived with
her husband seven years after her marriage,
and was a widow for eighty-four years.
LUKE 2:36–37

Today's Focus: Anna still serving in her old
age while resting in God's sovereignty.

Today's Insight: God's sovereignty keeps you
focused and faithful when sorrows strike.

Life is full of surprises. Just when we think we have it all
figured out and our plan is in place—WHAM!—unexpected happens, leaving our lives spinning out of control and
us wondering, *What now?* Life's surprises can be devastating,
especially when we are young.

Years ago, my cousin eventually married her high school boyfriend. But first, after high school they went off to college. Upon graduation, after seven years of "dating," they finally got married and moved to a small community in East Texas. They had their whole lives ahead of them. They adjusted quickly to their community; so much so, he was elected mayor!

They had their lives well mapped out until that fatal day. They had loaded their car with items needed for a long-awaited vacation and had stopped to fill up their car with gas. She made a quick trip to the restroom while her husband started pumping gas. Moments later, a car swerved to avoid an oncoming car, and his car struck the gas pump, resulting in a major explosion. As she came out of the restroom, she watched her husband burn to death. You cannot imagine her devastation.

In one moment her life forever changed. Life is often like that, isn't it? One minute we are doing well, money in the bank, paying our bills on time, healthy and happy, planning, and then suddenly, life happens and brings everything to a screeching halt. How we respond in those moments greatly determines the happiness of the rest of our life.

Have you ever played with an Etch-A-Sketch? What the knobs are in the hands of the user is what a brush is in the hands of an artist creating on canvas. We often do the same thing with our lives. We draw up our plans. We carefully list our life's goals and ambitions. We keep it in front of us, admiring our drawing. We take a step back, examining each detail, and then declare, "That's it. What a great plan! I'm set for success." Then out of nowhere, God comes along in his sovereignty and gives it a good shake, erasing all our plans, leaving us devastated and staring at a blank screen. It's hard to imagine in the moment that God has a better plan drawn up for us than what we drew.

It is often difficult to understand God's sovereignty at times, especially during a crisis or life reversal. We look around at our circumstances asking, "How could God let this happen? If he really loved me, he would have never let this happen to me."

Perhaps those were some of the questions asked by a woman named Anna. Luke mentions her in his account of the first Christmas. After introducing us to Simeon, he tells us about Anna, whose name means "grace." You may not be familiar with her because her story only involves three verses in the Bible.

What do we know about Anna? Luke tells us in 2:36, "There was also a prophetess, Anna, a daughter of Phanuel, of the tribe of Asher." She wasn't the only prophetess mentioned in the Bible. We're told in Acts 21:9 of Philip's four unmarried daughters who also had the gift of prophecy. A prophetess, like a prophet, was a person who, having received revelations of the mind and will of God, declared to others what had been received.[18] Anna knew the Word of God and could explain it in terms that common people could understand. She was a gift to the church.

Luke then tells us something about Anna you wouldn't expect: "She was well along in years, having lived with her husband seven years after her marriage, and was a widow for eighty-four years" (vv. 36–37). Either Luke didn't know her age or didn't want to ask. Even in the first century, a woman's age was a private matter after a certain point. My mother is currently ninety-two and doesn't hesitate to tell anyone and everyone. I'm not sure what magic number a woman decides where age is something to tell, but Anna was not even close.

In that day, the average Jewish girl married around the age of fifteen. If that were true of Anna, she would have been twenty-two years old when she became a widow. She and her husband were enjoying life, making plans, creating on their Etch-A-Sketch, when suddenly her drawing was erased. I can imagine her at her husband's funeral, emotionally spent as she watched him being buried, perhaps asking herself, *Why me? Why would God allow this to happen to me? Why now? Here I am at twenty-two years old with no husband to provide for me. I will live destitute the rest of my life.* Or perhaps she was thinking, *I know God loves me and has a plan for my life. I know the death of my husband hasn't caught God off guard. He will take care of me and meet all my needs. What is God wanting to teach me? What is he trying to say to me?*

Let me ask you this: Which response would you say is healthier? The *why* response which asks, "Why would God allow this if he loved me?" or the *what* response which asks, "Knowing that God loves me, what does he want to teach me?" I've learned over the years that I never get any answers to my *whys*, but I get many answers to my *whats*.

Griefs and sorrows can turn a person against God, depending on what they believe about his sovereignty. Show me a bitter person, and I'll show you someone who doesn't believe or understand the sovereignty of God. How did Anna experience great sorrow and grief without growing bitter? By resting in God's sovereignty. She trusted God's plan more than she trusted hers.

Perhaps you have experienced great grief and sorrow in your life. Have you ever considered your grief as a gift from God? If it drives you to God, it's a gift.

Today's Prayer: *Lord, help me better understand your sovereignty. I realize your plans are better than mine. As painful as it was, thank you for shaking the Etch-A-Sketch of my life and erasing my plans. Give me the faith to trust and follow you and to rest in your sovereignty. In Jesus's name, amen.*

She did not leave the temple, serving God
night and day with fasting and prayers.

LUKE 2:37

Today's Focus: Anna still serving in her old
age while resting in God's sovereignty.

Today's Insight: God's sovereignty is
a great motive for serving God.

Evelyn was an elderly woman in our church who had spent her life serving God. I suppose she had served in just about every area of the church over the past fifty years. As she grew older, she became confined to a wheelchair due to health issues, but her smile was still as bright as the morning sun.

One day as we were talking, she expressed her desire to continue serving God but didn't see how she could any more due to her age and physical restrictions. I asked her if she enjoyed talking on the phone. She said, "Pastor, what woman doesn't?" as she broke out in a smile the size of Texas. I asked her if I gave her the names and numbers on Monday of the people who had visited our church on Sunday, would she be willing to call and thank them for visiting, share a few things about our church, and pray with them. She said, "Absolutely. That can be my new ministry."

And for the next several years, the first person who contacted our Sunday guests was Evelyn. At the end of each week, she would give me an update and let me know if anyone she talked to needed a contact from me. Every pastor longs for members like Evelyn.

What are you dedicating your life to? Is it predominately to the temporary or the eternal? Here is a secret I learned years ago: *you have one life that will soon be past; only what's done for Christ will last.* Evelyn understood that truth and gave her life away serving others.

Anna the prophetess was like that too. After her husband died, she chose to spend the rest of her life giving it away in serving God. We're told in Luke 2:37 that she "was a widow for eighty-four years. She did not leave the temple, serving God night and day with fasting and prayers."

Being widowed at the age of twenty-two must have been challenging. Luke does not tell us anything about her husband. We don't know his name, his age, his occupation, or how he died. Nor does he tell us how Anna's needs were met—like where she lived, what she did for income, or if she had family nearby. All we are told is that she had been a widow for eighty-four years and continued serving God at the temple.

When Luke recorded his Christmas account, Anna would have been over a hundred years old and still serving God. She never let her age be an excuse for not serving God.

How are you serving God? Perhaps like Evelyn, you may have health issues limiting how you can serve. Maybe your age or health won't allow you to serve as you did previously, but it doesn't need to limit your service. Talk to your pastor or some other church leader and find out what the needs are. Chances are there are needs within your church fellowship only you can meet. There is work to do even for those who are "well along in years."

Do you know what kept Anna going to the temple every day to serve? She didn't want to miss the Messiah. Perhaps Anna knew the promise God made to Simeon about his not dying until he saw the Lord's Messiah. If so, she would have kept a close eye on Simeon, don't you think? She would be at the temple every time the doors were open, especially if she knew Simeon was going to be there, because she didn't want to miss the chance to see the Messiah.

Did you notice how Anna served God "with fasting and prayers" (v. 37)? She purposely went without food so she could spend more time in the temple. The Greek word for "prayers" could be translated "petitions." This is the kind of praying that asks things from God. Perhaps her prayers were like John's in Revelation 22:20: "Come, Lord Jesus!" She was fasting and praying for the fulfillment of his promises.

I love Luke 2:38: "At that very moment . . ." That is, at the very moment Simeon took the Lord's Messiah up in his arms, praising God and praying, Anna was there. She arrived right on time. I can see Anna observing Mary and Joseph placing their child in the arms of Simeon, and then hearing him break out in praise and prayer, thinking, *He is the one! The Lord's Messiah has come. God has fulfilled his promise to Simeon.* Don't you know Anna was glad she didn't skip church that day! It's aways good to be in church when Jesus shows up!

As Anna observed the child in Simeon's arms and having heard him bless Mary and Joseph, we read in verse 38 that Anna "came up and began to thank God and to speak about him to all who were looking forward to the redemption of Jerusalem." Those who encounter Jesus speak about him. Anna left the temple that day spreading the news of the newborn Savior.

As quickly as Anna appears in Scripture, she vanishes from its pages; three verses about an elderly widow who lived her life resting in God's sovereignty. The more she rested, the more her faith grew. The more her faith grew, the more her trust grew. The more her trust grew, the more certain she was of the promises of God. It's no wonder she never lost hope or the desire to serve.

What could have caused her to grow bitter (the loss of her husband) caused her to grow better because of what she believed about God. Don't let anyone ever tell you what you believe about God doesn't matter. What you believe about him determines how you survive life's storms.

Today's Prayer: *Lord, thank you for women like Anna who give me hope and remind me that my situation in life is no excuse for not serving you. Forgive me for the times when I've failed to serve your people and for allowing the devil a foothold in my life. My yes is on the table. I ask you to show me where to serve. In Jesus's name, amen.*

———————

DAY 22

"Do not be afraid, Mary, for you
have found favor with God."
LUKE 1:30

Today's Focus: Mary taken by surprise
at the sovereignty of God.

Today's Insight: God's sovereignty
is often filled with surprises.

When was the last time you were really surprised? Perhaps it was an unexpected gift from a loved one for no reason outside of their just thinking of you. Maybe it was a text from an old friend you hadn't heard from in years, or maybe it was something as simple as being offered an opportunity to visit with friends and family that was not planned. Surprises come in all shapes and sizes, some bad and some good. I don't know about you, but I prefer good surprises over bad ones. I have had my share of bad surprises, like the day I was told I had a fast-growing malignant cancer in my throat. That was a bad day that changed my life moving forward. That's how surprises are, aren't they? Whether they are good or bad, surprises are often life-changing.

I suppose one of the biggest surprises I ever had involved my fortieth birthday. My wife worked months arranging all the details while I remained clueless. She reserved a large ballroom at the local country club with special hors d'oeuvres. She took pictures of me growing up and enlarged them, creating posters to set up throughout the ballroom. She invited guests who were a part of my childhood. She requested video birthday greetings from various pastors and leaders from across the country to show during the party.

On top of that, she was in cahoots with our worship leader to create a scenario that called for me to go with him to the country club that evening. As we walked in, several hundred people stood to their feet, singing "Happy Birthday"! It was an evening of shock and awe, which would have never happened without my wife orchestrating it all.

Who doesn't like a good surprise? Mary, the mother of Jesus, reminds us today that God's sovereignty is often filled with surprises. Think of them as "sovereignty surprises." Some of them are pleasant and welcoming, while others are unpleasant and unwelcoming. But he allows both kinds of surprises within his sovereignty for our good and his glory.

In Luke 1 we read about a young girl named Mary who experienced a sovereignty surprise one day from an angel sent by God. She was told she was going to have a child. And not just any child, but a male child. And not just any male child, but the Son of God. I'd call that a sovereignty surprise!

Then she was told in verses 32–33: "He will be great and will be called the Son of the Most High, and the Lord God will give him the throne of his father David. He will reign over the house of Jacob forever, and his kingdom will have no end."

Luke mentions another sovereignty surprise: Mary was a virgin and engaged to be married. Talk about a village scandal! It would have been easy for Mary to run and hide. She even could have aborted the baby! I imagine Mary considered all her options; who wouldn't? It didn't take her long to realize that this was a sovereignty surprise, and she was the recipient.

You've got to love this conversation between Mary and Gabriel, God's angel of good news. Mary asked her angelic visitor, "How can this be, since I have not had sexual relations with a man?" (v. 34). The angel told her, "The Holy Spirit will come upon you, and the power of the Most High will overshadow you" (v. 35).

Maybe you need a sovereignty surprise in your life, the kind of surprise that will forever change your life's direction. Let me show you what I believe is the secret to receiving such a surprise from God. It is found in verse 28 when Gabriel first approached Mary: "Greetings, favored woman! The Lord is with you." And then in verse 30, the angel said, "Do not be afraid, Mary, for you have found favor with God."

The favor of God was upon Mary's life. That's not to say she was the only one on the earth at the time experiencing God's favor. Mary was likely one of many. Would you say God's favor is upon your life? Do you know what favor means? The favor of God is the grace of God. This word is sometimes translated *good will* or *favor*, but most often it is simply *grace*. That means today God extends his grace or favor to you.

That raises another question: What is grace? Grace is God giving you something you don't deserve. And in God's grace you will find his love, his forgiveness, his salvation, and so much more! Without God's grace, you have no salvation. Without salvation, you have no hope. The Bible tells us in Ephesians 2:5, "You are saved by grace!" And then in verse 8, "For you are saved by grace through faith, and this is not from yourselves;"—now watch this—"it is God's gift."

I suppose God's greatest sovereignty surprise in my life was the day he came into my life and saved me. Holy God loved someone like me enough to send his only Son Jesus to shed his blood and die on a cross to pay my sin debt. The Bible tells us in Romans 5:8, "But God proves his own love for us in that while we were still sinners, Christ died for us."

Do you see the word *for* in that verse? It speaks of a substitute. Here is what that means for us today: Jesus died as our substitute or in our place so that we might live forever with him. You may be thinking that you are beyond God's grace or favor because of the choices you have made, that your sin is greater than God's grace. May I let you in on a sovereignty surprise today? God still loves you. His grace is greater than your sin. You can experience his grace by experiencing his Son. The Bible tells us in 2 Peter 3:9 that God "is patient with you, not wanting any to perish but all to come to repentance."

Aren't you glad Mary chose to have her Baby? Aren't you glad she listened to the word of God that day brought by an angel, God's messenger? Have you experienced God's greatest sovereignty surprise? It is available to you today by his grace.

Today's Prayer: *Lord, thank you for hearing my prayer today. As I learn to rest in your sovereignty, remind me that your favor is available in my life as I call upon you to forgive and save me. Your grace saves and strengthens me. May your favor fuel my faith as I face my challenges today. In Jesus's name, amen.*

DAY 23

"For nothing will be impossible with God."

LUKE 1:37

Today's Focus: Mary's surprise at
the sovereignty of God.

Today's Insight: God's sovereignty is
often filled with the impossible.

I grew up in the early 1970s watching the television series *Mission Impossible.* Some of you probably didn't even know it was ever a television series, but it was. If you don't believe me, google it. You will find that Jim Phelps was the head of a supersecret government agency, the I.M.F. (Impossible Missions Force), and was given secret, anonymous, covert missions subject to official denial in the event of failure, death, or capture.

Every week I sat in front of our black-and-white Zenith television with rabbit ears on top (some of you might have to google that as well) with great anticipation to see what the impossible mission was and how Jim Phelps and his partner Barney Collier would solve it, and they did every week.

That television series was so successful it won nineteen Emmy awards and had thirty-nine nominations, and became a springboard for seven *Mission Impossible* movies starting in 1996 with the eighth one scheduled to be released in the summer of 2024. Hollywood can solve any impossible mission with enough time and money and some good writers. But what Hollywood produces is fantasy, not real life, where we live.

Have you ever faced an impossible mission? Perhaps you're facing one today. It may be an impossible health situation or an impossible financial situation or an impossible relationship situation. You're looking at your impossible situation and thinking:

"I will never _____."

"It's impossible for me to _____."

"Our marriage will never _____."

"Our child will never _____."

When the angel came to Mary and told her in Luke 1:31, "You will conceive and give birth to a son, and you will name him Jesus," you can know that Mary's immediate thought was, *That's impossible!* She asked in verse 34, "How can this be, since I have not had sexual relations with a man?" In other words, what the angel was declaring to her was physically impossible. She was a virgin and virgins don't have children. Certainly, this angel must have made a mistake.

Earlier in the chapter, the angel Gabriel had visited Zechariah and Elizabeth, announcing they were going to have a child in their old age. It's one thing to have a child in old age; it is something else entirely to have a child when you're a virgin. Elizabeth's impossibility was just God's warm-up act for what was about to happen to Mary. The impossible was about to happen! Mary was not only going to have a son, but the Son of God!

The key to Mary's encounter with Gabriel is in verse 37 when he told her, "For nothing will be impossible with God." Do you see the last two words, *with God*? That's the secret that unlocks the door of the impossible becoming possible. Not with man. Not with your doctor. Not with your financial consultant. But the impossible becomes possible with God. When God becomes your source, start looking for the impossible to become possible.

Allow me to show you another Bible verse which speaks to your current and future impossible situation. It's found in Jeremiah 32:26–27: "The word of the LORD came to Jeremiah: 'Look, I am the LORD, the God over every creature. Is anything too difficult for me?'" Do you see the word *anything*? Place your finger over that word and read the passage again.

"Is _____ too difficult for me?"

Let's make it more personal. When you remove your finger, the word *anything* reappears. God asks, "Is anything too difficult for me?" Now think about the impossible mission you're facing and replace the word *anything* with your impossible situation.

"Is _____ too difficult for me?"

Whatever you place in the blank is not too difficult for God. In other words, nothing is too difficult for him. Nothing! Not your impossible situation. Not my impossible situation. Not any impossible situation.

The Hebrew text literally says, "No, absolutely nothing for you is extraordinary or surpassing." The text begins with the strongest negative known in the Hebrew language. "No, nothing, absolutely nothing for You, LORD, is extraordinary."[19] God specializes in things thought impossible. He does the things others cannot do.

Did you notice how God set up this statement to Jeremiah in the first half of verse 27 when he said, "Look, I am the LORD, the God over every creature"? Before he tells Jeremiah that nothing is too difficult for him, God reminds him that he is sovereign, that he is over every creature. Don't miss this: because he is the sovereign God, he is the supplying God. He supplies what is needed to meet your impossible situation. The impossible becomes possible when you have a sovereign God.

Need more convincing? Consider the words of Jesus spoken to the rich young ruler in Luke 18:27: "What is impossible with man is possible with God." That truth makes me want to stand on a chair and shout *Hallelujah!* Read it again slowly, "What is impossible with man is possible with God." There's a Bible verse worthy of memorizing.

Nothing is impossible with God! Say it out loud: "Nothing is impossible with God." You say, "But Ernest, God hasn't stepped into my impossible situation and changed it." Not yet. But consider this. It's not your situation God wants to change, but you. Remember, you are a sovereign vessel, as R. T. Kendall explains, earmarked by God for a special work far beyond what you're doing at the moment.[20] God allows us to face impossible situations to do a work in us that makes us more like Jesus.

It may be time to change our praying from "Lord, help me as I go through this impossible situation; please change it" to "Lord, help me as I go through this impossible situation; please change me."

Today's Prayer: *Lord, thank you that I can trust you today with my impossible situation. If it is within your sovereign will, I ask that you will make my impossible situation possible. And if not, use it to change me and make me more like you. Whatever the outcome, I thank you in advance for working in my life today to deepen my faith and trust in you. In Jesus's name, amen.*

DAY 24

Peter told him [Jesus], "Even if everyone falls
away because of you, I will never fall away."
MATTHEW 26:33

Today's Focus: Peter's failure and God's sovereignty.

Today's Insight: Peter's failure was
predicted within God's sovereignty.

A man who was losing his memory went to his doctor for
advice. After a careful examination, the doctor said, "We
cannot help your memory without impairing your eyesight.
The choice is yours. Would you rather be able to see or to
remember?" The man thought about it for a moment and
said, "Sir, I would rather see where I am going than remember
where I have been."[21] This man reminds us that our future is

more important than our past. No matter how hard you try, you cannot unscramble an egg. Failure is like that, isn't it? It is the gift that keeps on giving.

Failure, if not handled correctly, can rob you of God's best for you. Failure seems to weave itself into the fabric of our lives. A failed test. A failed grade. A failed marriage. A failed business. A failed dream. You might be thinking now, *I feel like such a failure.*

Perhaps growing up, you were told over and over what a failure you were, and now you are grown and convinced you are. Perhaps your failure has you believing you're somehow a second-class saint and your days of usefulness are gone. Maybe the devil has convinced you that God doesn't use failures, that God has no place for failures in his plans.

In *The Screwtape Letters*, C. S. Lewis described the strategy Satan's demons use and said, "He gets Christians to become preoccupied with their failures; from then on, the battle is won."[22] It may surprise you, but the Bible is full of failures. I suppose one of the most famous Bible failures was a man named Simon Peter. In fact, his biggest failure is recorded in all four Gospel accounts. Aren't you glad your biggest failure hasn't been read, discussed, and taught to every generation during the last two thousand years? It's bad enough when those closest to us know about it.

To make matters worse, Jesus predicted Peter's failure. After Peter boldly tells him in Matthew 26:33 that he would never deny him, Jesus quickly says in verse 34, "Tonight, before the rooster crows, you will deny me three times." You want to guess what happened? Just as Jesus said, Peter denied knowing Jesus three times when faced with the pressure of persecution.

Failure is devastating, especially a spiritual one. It's one thing to fail in our professional or personal lives, but to fail spiritually takes our failure to the next level. Perhaps you have recently experienced a spiritual failure. It could have been that person you refused to forgive, or that fellow believer you just won't love, or that lost person God spoke to you about sharing Jesus with and you refused. Spiritual failures come in a variety of ways.

Here's the good news from the life of Peter: failures are fatal only if we fail to learn from them![23] I find it less painful to learn from the failure of others than my own failures. Take, for example, Simon Peter. What can we learn from his failures and how to overcome them?

First, he remembered the words of Jesus. We read in Matthew 26:75: "Peter remembered the words Jesus had spoken." When failure strikes, don't forget the Word! Don't forget Isaiah 1:18: "'Come, let's settle this,' says the LORD. 'Though your sins are scarlet, they will be as white as snow; though they are crimson red, they will be like wool.'"

Don't forget Romans 8:38–39: "For I am persuaded that neither death nor life, nor angels nor rulers, nor things present nor things to come, nor powers, nor height nor depth, nor any other created thing will be able to separate us from the love of God that is in Christ Jesus our Lord." Don't forget the Word!

Second, he recognized his failure. We read in Matthew 26:75: "And he went outside and wept bitterly." Those were tears of sorrow and brokenness. He didn't attempt to cover up his failure; he openly confessed it. The Bible says in Proverbs 28:13, "The one who conceals his sins will not prosper, but whoever confesses and renounces them will find mercy."

You will never overcome failure without confession and repentance. There is something incredibly powerful and releasing in those three words, *I was wrong.* No defense. No excuses. No rationalizing. No blaming others. But simply owning your own sin and following the promise of 1 John 1:9: "If we confess our sins, he is faithful and righteous to forgive us our sins and to cleanse us from all unrighteousness." It is a part of overcoming failure.

Third, he remained with the group. We find in John 21:1–3: "After this, Jesus revealed himself again to his disciples by the Sea of Tiberias. He revealed himself in this way: Simon Peter, Thomas (called "Twin"), Nathanael from Cana of Galilee, Zebedee's sons, and two others of his disciples were together. 'I'm going fishing,' Simon Peter said to them. 'We're coming with you,' they told him. They went out and got into the boat, but that night they caught nothing."

Seven friends, seven followers of Jesus, went fishing together. Here is one Bible principle for overcoming failure: surround yourself with people who love God. Don't isolate. Judas isolated himself from the group after failure and hung himself.

After you fail, stay in the group with the rest of the people who fail too. That is what Peter did, and that's how he overcame his failure. Think about a bunch of bananas. The only one that gets peeled is the one that leaves the bunch. And so will you.

Today's Prayer: *Lord, forgive me of my past failures. Thank you for the gift of the body of Christ to journey with me as I overcome my failures. Help me learn from them and use them as stepping stones to the victorious Christian life. In Jesus's name, amen.*

DAY 25

*When they had eaten breakfast, Jesus
asked Simon Peter, "Simon, son of John,
do you love me more than these?"*

JOHN 21:15

Today's Focus: Peter's failure and God's sovereignty.

Today's Insight: Peter's restoration was
possible within God's sovereignty.

H ave you ever enjoyed watching someone fail? Perhaps it
was another athlete competing for your position who
missed the winning tackle. Or maybe another student whose
grade point average was edging you out of graduating at the
top of your class bombed the final exam. Or another employee
whom the company was considering promoting was caught

embezzling, which opened the door for you to get promoted. Their failure made it possible for your advancement.

If we are honest, we would all probably admit to finding pleasure in someone else's failure. It makes us feel better about ourselves. As they fall, we climb up. Something within our fallen nature likes it. You may have never thought about it, but when we gloat over the failure of others, we are failing and denying Jesus, who said in John 13:34–35: "I give you a new command: Love one another. Just as I have loved you, you are also to love one another. By this everyone will know that you are my disciples, if you love one another."

If anyone was gloating over Peter's failure of denying Jesus three times, it didn't last long because within hours all of Jesus's disciples deserted and failed him. Every one of them. They all scattered like turkeys at the first sound of gunfire. So, when we experience spiritual failure, we are in good company. If Simon Peter's failure teaches us anything, it teaches us that no failure is too great for God's grace to restore.

All four Gospel accounts record Peter's failure, but only one records his restoration. You can read about it in John 21. Take a moment and slowly read through the first 19 verses. This may be one of the most tender encounters of Jesus with one of his disciples in all the Bible record. John recorded it just for us.

Peter miserably failed Jesus through his denials. And hours later, Jesus was nailed to a cross after being flogged and humiliated in public. Three days pass, and Jesus is resurrected from the dead. A group of women find his tomb empty. Jesus, in his resurrected body, appears to several individuals and groups. In great despair and defeat, Peter and a few of his friends head back to the Galilee, and in verse 3, Peter tells them, "I'm going fishing."

After fishing all night and catching nothing, we read in verses 4–6: "When daybreak came, Jesus stood on the shore, but the disciples did not know it was Jesus. 'Friends,' Jesus called to them, 'you don't have any fish, do you?' 'No,' they answered.' 'Cast the net on the right side of the boat,' he told them, 'and you'll find some.'"

They did as he suggested, and they caught so many fish "they were unable to haul it in" (v. 6). Verse 7 tells us: "The disciple, the one Jesus loved [probably a reference to John], said to Peter, 'It is the Lord!'"

Peter, in an act of impulsion, dove in the water and swam to shore. When he and the other disciples arrived, we read in verse 9: "They saw a charcoal fire there, with fish lying on it, and bread." They proceeded to have breakfast with Jesus.

The phrase "charcoal fire" is used only one other time in Scripture, and that is in John 18:18, when the officials were warming themselves and "Peter was standing with them, warming himself." By that charcoal fire, Peter denied knowing Jesus. Now in John 21, as Peter the failure swam to shore, the first thing he saw was another "charcoal fire." Can you imagine the emotions racing through his soul seeing that fire? Do you think it reminded him of his failure?

But this charcoal fire, unlike the other one, was not a fire of rejection but a fire of restoration. The risen Jesus was there determined to restore this fallen saint back into fellowship with his Savior.

This awkward conversation began with Jesus asking Peter, "Do you love me more than these?" (v. 15). In fact, three times Jesus asked Peter if he loved him, once for every failure. Each time, Peter responded, "You know that I love you" (vv. 15–17).

Remember today that Jesus is in the business of restoring failures. Perhaps like Peter, you love and follow Jesus. But like Peter, you have wandered away from fellowship with him. Peter failed God, leaving Peter devastated and discouraged. What Peter needed that day is what you need this day, and that is restoration.

God tells us in Hosea 11:7: "My people are bent on turning from me." Yes, we are bent on backsliding. We are bent on going back to our old way of living and thinking before we were saved. As the hymn says, we are "prone to wander, Lord I feel it, prone to leave the God I love."[24]

Do you know what Jesus wanted to know from backslidden Peter? If he truly loved him. Jesus could have asked, "Peter, are you sorry?" He could have asked, "Peter, do you want another chance?" He could have asked, "Peter, you were full of pride and denied me! What do you have to say for yourself?"

But instead, Jesus asked this failure and every failure since then, "Do you love me?" What God blesses more than anything is your love for Jesus. Not your efforts. Not your service. Not your actions. What God blesses more than all those things is your love for Jesus.

There is room for failure within the sovereignty of God. God's sovereignty decreed that man should be free to exercise moral choice, and man from the beginning has fulfilled that decree by making his choice between good and evil. When he chooses to do evil, he does not thereby countervail the sovereign will of God, but fulfills it. Man's will is free because God is sovereign. A God less than sovereign could not bestow moral freedom upon his creatures. He would be afraid to do so.[25]

Today's Prayer: *Lord, forgive me for my failures. I'm grateful that within your sovereignty there is hope for failures. Give me more grace as I overcome past failures and look forward to future victories. I truly love you. In Jesus's name, amen.*

DAY 26

"Therefore let all the house of Israel know with
certainty that God has made this Jesus, whom
you crucified, both Lord and Messiah."
ACTS 2:36

Today's Focus: Peter's failure and God's sovereignty.

Today's Insight: Peter's restoration positioned
him within God's sovereignty for usefulness.

The grief of failure and the gladness of restoration. It's the in-between time we find so gut-wrenching. I'm talking about that period after we fail God until the moment he restores us. We don't feel right deep within our soul as the Holy Spirit begins convicting and confronting us with our sin. It's painful. Solomon described it in Proverbs 20:17: "Food gained by fraud is sweet to a person, but afterward his mouth is full of gravel." I admit I've never had a mouthful of gravel, but just the thought of it sounds extremely unpleasant.

Don't you know that Peter wondered if the day would ever come when his in-between time would come to an end, if the pain he was experiencing would ever stop. Perhaps that is how you feel today. You have sowed the wind, and now you're reaping the whirlwind. Your fellowship with God has been damaged by your choices. You are wondering if the day will ever come when your fellowship with God is restored. You personally know the answer to the question asked by the prophet Amos: "Can two walk together without agreeing to meet?" (Amos 3:3). The answer is a resounding no!

I have some wonderful news to give you. Are you ready? Here it is: God has never met a sinner he didn't love or couldn't save or couldn't restore. That includes you! Do you want some even better news? You say, "Ernest, how could there be better news than knowing God has never met a sinner he didn't love or couldn't save or couldn't restore?" There is and it's this: that includes you! God loves you and can save you and restore you. In the midst of your failure, here is what God wants to know: "Do you love my Son, Jesus?"

During the times I have failed, the first thing I want to do is to work harder, to read my Bible more, to give more, to memorize more Scripture—as though doing those things would help remove the pain of my failure. But as we saw yesterday, during those times we fail, what Jesus wants to know is if we love him.

How a leader handles failure (or feelings of failure) will set much of the agenda for the future. Peter appeared washed up as a leader after his denial of Christ, but repentance and love reopened the door of opportunity, and Peter's leadership touched all the rest of Christendom.[26] Let me briefly mention three benefits of experiencing restoration from God.

First, restoration straightens out your issues with God. Until you get right with God, you're not going to be right with anyone. The Bible says in 1 John 1:9, "If we confess our sins, he is faithful and righteous to forgive us our sins and to cleanse us from all unrighteousness." God stands ready to forgive and cleanse you, restoring your fellowship with him. You can say along with Paul in Acts 23:1, "I have lived my life before God in all good conscience to this day." That "day" can begin for you "this day."

Second, restoration strengthens you to accomplish great things for God. After Jesus restored his fellowship with Peter and now with his failure behind him, Peter found strength to move beyond his failure. You may be able to accomplish some good things in the flesh while living in a broken fellowship with Jesus, but you cannot accomplish any great things without a restored fellowship with him.

Third, restoration supplies you with the power needed to do more than you ever thought possible. Do you know when Peter and the other disciples moved to another level? Having been restored with Jesus, we then find Peter gathered in an upper room in Jerusalem, waiting for the arrival of the Holy Spirit. Acts 1:13 says, "When they arrived, they went to the room upstairs where they were staying." And the first person named? You guessed it: restored Peter! For ten days they remained in that upper room. Verse 14 tells us, "They were all continually united in prayer, along with the women, including Mary the mother of Jesus, and his brothers."

Then, on the day of Pentecost, while in that room, we read in Acts 2:4: "Then they were all filled with the Holy Spirit." Don't miss the sequence. After Peter was restored by Jesus, he was then filled with the Holy Spirit. And once he was filled with the Holy Spirit, he never looked back. He now had a holy boldness he lacked in the flesh. Beginning in Acts 2:14, Peter went on to preach a Holy Spirit-filled message quoting the prophet Joel and King David and concluded his message in verse 36 by declaring: "Therefore let all the house of Israel know with certainty that God has made this Jesus, whom you crucified, both Lord and Messiah."

No fear of the authorities. No hesitancy in publicly declaring Jesus. No shrinking back from declaring the Word of God. Just straightforward and all-in. Restoration + a Holy Spirit filling = a powerful tool in the hand of God. Let me say it another way: there is no Holy Spirit living without first being restored to God. And there is no restoration without repentance (turning away from our sin and turning back to God).

The Bible says in Ephesians 5:18: "be filled by the Spirit." The Holy Spirit cannot fill what is not empty. We must first empty ourselves from all sin through confession and repentance before the Holy Spirit can fill us. We do the emptying, and he does the filling.

Today's Prayer: *Lord, I'm tired of living in our broken fellowship. I realize my choices have driven a wedge between us, and I ask you to forgive and cleanse and restore me to yourself. Please forgive me of all my sin, and fill me with your Holy Spirit. May I live with a holy boldness to declare the truth of your Word regardless of the circumstances. In Jesus's name, amen.*

===============

DAY 27

"Are you the one who is to come, or
should we expect someone else?"

MATTHEW 11:3

Today's Focus: John the Baptist looking for
answers regarding God's sovereignty.

Today's Insight: John's doubts
drive him to Jesus (part 1).

Have you ever doubted God? It might have occurred during
a crisis of belief. You may sometimes feel like C. S. Lewis
who said, "Often when I pray I wonder if I am not posting
letters to a non-existent address. Mind you, I don't *think* so—
the whole of my reasonable mind is convinced: but I often *feel*
so."[27] Doubts come in a variety of ways:

Doubting God's existence

Doubting God's forgiveness

Doubting God's love

Doubting God's acceptance

Doubting God's salvation

I have a friend who often doubts his salvation. One day he believes he is saved, and the next day he's not so sure. His struggle reminds me that we have a busy enemy; if he cannot shut us out of heaven, he will try hard to make our journey uncomfortable.[28] Many followers of Jesus are just like my friend. Perhaps you are one of them.

In a recent discussion with him regarding his doubts, I shared my own experience. I came to know Christ at the tender age of nine. I grew up in a Bible-believing church that loved me, and I learned from them how God loved me and had a plan for my life. I was at church on Sunday mornings and on Sunday and Wednesday evenings. I participated in every summer camp and vacation Bible school. I sang in the youth choir and was involved in our church's Royal Ambassador program. I was all in. But deep inside, where no one could see, I experienced some nagging doubts regarding my salvation. Had God really saved me?

Age helps give perspective. As I have thought through that time in my life, I finally realized the cause of my doubts. I don't think our church taught what I'm about to tell you, but it is what I came to understand. I understood that because I was now a follower of Jesus, certain thoughts and actions that should be gone since I was now "saved."

I hadn't been saved very long when I realized I still had some of the same thoughts and actions. I looked around and thought, *If I was really saved, these thoughts and actions would no longer be in my heart and mind.* But they were, and as a result, doubts arose. Like many today, I was confused. I felt like the apostle Paul when he said in Romans 7:15: "I do not practice what I want to do, but I do what I hate," and again in verse 19, "For I do not do the good that I want to do, but I practice the evil that I do not want to do," and finally in verse 24, "What a wretched man I am! Who will rescue me from this body of death?" Perhaps you can identify with Paul too.

Living the Christian life, for me, was a matter of dos and don'ts. If I was truly saved, I wouldn't have certain thoughts; I wouldn't do certain things. I couldn't be saved! But I was. I know I was saved because I was there when it happened.

My struggle came down to this: I was trying to change from the outside in, rather than allowing Jesus to change me from the inside out. I was following the path of the Pharisees, which was the road of legalism. Here's what I soon discovered: I couldn't change me. If I kept depending on my thoughts and actions to confirm my salvation, I was in trouble.

Over the years, I've discovered that the key to removing spiritual doubts is including Christian disciplines in our life that draw us closer to Jesus. The closer we get to Jesus, doubts seem to dissolve. Spiritual disciplines are like physical disciplines; they develop us spiritually into solid men and women of God.

Spiritual disciplines are doubt dissolvers. I'm talking about disciplines such as daily Bible reading, daily prayer time, daily worship, Bible memorization, giving, fasting, and witnessing. Once these disciplines are part of your life, you will look around one day and wonder where all your doubts went. Jesus is the doubt remover. Remember, we don't change from the outside in; Jesus changes us from the inside out. Some people call that process *sanctification*. It's a process that will continue until we one day step into heaven.

When you think about doubters in the Bible, who is the first person who comes to mind? Let me guess: Thomas? It's true, Thomas doubted the resurrection of Jesus but soon came around when Jesus showed up, asking him if he wanted to touch his wounds. Then Thomas declared in John 20:28: "My Lord and my God!"

Yes. Thomas had doubts. But did you know the one of whom Jesus declared, "Among those born of women no one greater than John the Baptist has appeared" (Matt. 11:11), had his own doubts too? John asked Jesus, "Are you the one who is to come, or should we expect someone else?" (v. 3). If the greatest person born of women had doubts, don't be surprised when you do.

Today's Prayer: *Lord, you know all about my doubts. With every effort I put forth to change, I seem to dig deeper into the pit of doubt. Today I quit trying and begin trusting you.*

Rather than focusing on what I'm doing or not doing, I am implementing spiritual disciplines to draw me closer to you. Thank you for your grace in my life. In Jesus's name, amen.

———————

DAY 28

"Are you the one who is to come, or
should we expect someone else?"
Matthew 11:3

Today's Focus: John the Baptist looking for
answers regarding God's sovereignty.

Today's Insight: John's doubts
drive him to Jesus (part 2).

Doubts are like prisons. They rob us of the freedom we
have in Christ. They isolate us and eventually suffocate
us, believing there are no answers to remove our doubts. With
every doubt we have, God seems to get a little farther away
from us. And we go on living in the dungeon of defeat and
doubt.

What doubts keep you trapped in the dungeon of defeat? Perhaps you feel like the person who said, "There have been nights when I literally scream at God, pleading for some signal that he is real." John the Baptist had nights like that, and he was, according to Jesus, the greatest person ever born of women.

Maybe you are thinking, *If God is sovereign, how could one of his children have doubts about him or about what he has allowed to come their way?* One thing we can learn from John the Baptist is that there is room for doubts in the kingdom our God rules. The sovereignty of God isn't a guarantee of a trouble-free, doubt-free life; rather, it is the guarantee of God's rule.

In Matthew 11 we find John confined to prison, facing death at any moment. According to Mathew 14:3–5: "Herod had arrested John, chained him, and put him in prison on account of Herodias, his brother Philip's wife, since John had been telling him, 'It's not lawful for you to have her.' Though Herod wanted to kill John, he feared the crowd since they regarded John as a prophet." John was imprisoned for addressing the wickedness of King Herod Antipas.

Step into John's prison cell with me for a moment. There in that dark, damp, and dreary dungeon sits one of God's greatest prophets, chained. He is hungry, thirsty, and physically exhausted from lack of sleep. It has been weeks, if not longer, since he bathed. The stench of human waste lingers in the air. Sitting there, perhaps he remembers the words of Jesus in John 16:33: "You will have suffering in this world. Be courageous! I have conquered the world." Or Matthew 10:22: "You will be hated by everyone because of my name. But the one who endures to the end will be saved." Or verse 24: "A disciple is not above his teacher, or a slave above his master."

There he sits, reflecting and remembering what he had previously heard Jesus say. Then, suddenly, he stands to his feet, looking upward, and says, "What if Jesus isn't your Son, sent to save sinners? What if he isn't the Messiah? I baptized him, believing he was the Lamb you sent to be offered as a blood sacrifice for the remission of sin. Here I am in this dungeon, probably going to be executed for believing in and following someone who may be a fraud."

John needed his doubts addressed, so he sent a message to Jesus, asking, "Are you the one who is to come, or should we expect someone else?" (Matt. 11:3). In other words, "I'm not dying for a fraud. I'm not dying for a lie. If you've been pretending these last few years, I need to know it now."

I don't know what dungeon of doubt you find yourself in today, but may I suggest that you do with your doubt what John did with his: take it to Jesus! John's doubts drove him to Jesus, where he found his answer. Matthew records Jesus's doubt-defying reply starting in Matthew 11:4–6: "Go and report to John what you hear and see: The blind receive their sight, the lame walk, those with leprosy are cleansed, the deaf hear, the dead are raised, and the poor are told the good news, and blessed is the one who isn't offended by me."

When John heard that, he had his answer. John knew the Old Testament prophecies concerning the Messiah. And when

Jesus's answer included a direct reference to Isaiah 35:5–6, his doubts dissolved like sugar in a hot cup of tea.

Jesus was saying, "John, you need assuring and proof that I am the Messiah. Here are some of the things I've been doing, just like the prophet Isaiah declared, which proves who I am." And then he adds: "Blessed is the one who isn't offended by me" (Matt. 11:6). The word *offended* can also be translated "repelled." In other words, "Blessed are those who do not allow anything I do or say to lure them into sin."

John the Baptist wasn't the only Baptist to have doubts about Jesus. Even the great ones have them. You may be in a season of spiritual doubt. You may not be in a prison, but your doubts are just as real as John's. Be encouraged today. Remember the words of Tim Stafford: "Doubt; broken faith, like broken bones, can grow back stronger."[29]

In the meantime, take your doubts to Jesus and let him give you an answer. I promise he has already given you the answer to your doubts. As with John, the answer he needed was recorded seven hundred years before he doubted. Jesus resolved John's doubt by taking him to the Word of God. Isn't that just like God? He provides the solution long before we ever have the need.

Today's Prayer: *Lord, I have been looking for the answers to my doubts in about every place except in your Word. Thank you in advance for resolving my doubt issues. Give me direction as I search your Word for the truth that will set me free. In Jesus's name, amen.*

DAY 29

*No one has ever seen God. The one and
only Son, who is himself God and is at the
Father's side—he has revealed him.*

JOHN 1:18

Today's Focus: Jesus fulfilling the
sovereignty of his Father.

Today's Insight: Jesus came to reveal God the Father.

D o you have a mission in life? I'm talking about something you live for. You wake up each morning thinking about it. It consumes your thoughts, attention, and focus. It impacts the decisions you make each day, how you spend your money and time. It is what you believe you were put on earth to accomplish. Can you describe your mission in one or two sentences? Finish this sentence: The mission of my life is to _____. Take a moment and write it down.

People with a mission are focused and driven. They tend to be less sidetracked with nonessentials. Henry Kaiser said, "Determine what you want more than anything else in life, write down the means by which you intend to attain it, and permit nothing to deter you from pursuing it."[30]

A person without a mission is like a ship's captain without reference points or someone on a long road trip without signs and mileposts. It's been said, "If you don't know what you're aiming for, you will hit it every time."

For Abraham Lincoln, the need to achieve was more than just a simple inclination; it was an almost uncontrollable obsession. His law partner, William Herndon, noted that he was "always calculating and planning ahead."[31] Did you catch that last phrase? "Always calculating and planning ahead." That is how people on mission live each day. They are driven by their mission.

Jesus was like that. He was always calculating and looking ahead. That is why you sometimes read in the Bible where he says, "Don't tell anyone what you have seen," because he knew the timing wasn't right. Jesus was mission driven. But rather than driven by his mission, he was driven by his Father's mission. In the first chapter of John's Gospel, we read in verse 14: "The Word became flesh and dwelt among us. We observed his glory, the glory as the one and only Son from the Father, full of grace and truth."

Have you ever wondered why the Word (Jesus) became flesh and dwelt among us? It boils down to this: because Jesus was on a mission, the mission of his life. And that mission was to reveal his Father. John explains that in verse 18: "No one has ever seen God. The one and only Son, who is himself God and is at the Father's side—he has revealed him." There it is! The life mission of Jesus was to reveal his Father.

What does it mean when the Bible says that Jesus "has revealed him"? Sometimes it helps to read other translations of the Bible to better understand a certain verse. For example, John 1:18, when John says that Jesus "has revealed him." Another translation says, "He has declared Him" (NKJV). Still another one says, "[He] has made him known" (NIV).

Here are three translations of John 1:18:

"He has revealed him."

"He has declared Him." (NKJV)

"[He] has made him known." (NIV)

The Greek word used by John is translated *exegete*. This word speaks of informing or describing or revealing. When used to describe the mission of Jesus, it means that Jesus has made this God, who has never been seen, to be seen. That is, Jesus gives us all the information we need to know about God, making our salvation possible.

That's how Jesus could say in John 14:9: "The one who has seen me has seen the Father." That's how the writer of Hebrews could say in Hebrews 1:3: "The Son is the radiance of God's glory and the exact expression of his nature, sustaining all things by his powerful word." Jesus is the great revealer!

The life mission of Jesus was to reveal or make his Father known to us. In Jesus, more is revealed about holy God than anything we read in the Old Testament. Throughout the Old Testament, we find pictures and shadows and descriptions that teach us truths about God, but in Jesus all those truths are crystallized to help us know more about him. Through Jesus we see the invisible God.

Once a person comes into a relationship with God through Jesus, resting in his sovereignty is made possible. Throughout the Scriptures, the theme of God's sovereignty is repeatedly presented as a comfort to believers. We need "be anxious for nothing" (Phil. 4:6 NKJV) because our heavenly Father reigns over all. He is all-powerful, all-wise, and all-present, and he has promised to work all things together for his glory and our good (Rom. 8:28). We have nothing to fear because if God is for us, who can be against us?[32] Keep in mind what the psalmist says in Psalm 115:3: "Our God is in heaven and does whatever he pleases." Here is what that means: we can trust him and rest in that reality. There is no resting without a relationship with Jesus.

God's sovereignty is grace driven. He rules and reigns by grace. By that same grace he saves. Here's what that means for us today: if we want to know what God is like, then look at Jesus. If we want to know what Jesus is like, look at his followers.

Today's Prayer: *Lord, I'm grateful for the life mission of Jesus to reveal more of you to me. You have changed and continue to change my life as I discover more about Jesus. Because of Jesus, I know you are good and caring and want to come into my life, forgive my sins, and give me peace. I'm grateful my life is under the control of your sovereign rule. In Jesus's name, amen.*

===========

*"My food is to do the will of him who
sent me and to finish his work."*

JOHN 4:34

Today's Focus: Jesus fulfilling the
sovereignty of his Father.

Today's Insight: Jesus came to redeem all mankind.

During the last month, we have focused on what it means to rest in God's sovereignty through the lives of several Old Testament and New Testament figures. Like us, they all had their own spiritual ups and downs, victories and failures, highs and lows. There were days that resting in God's sovereignty was challenging, seemingly impossible, and other days when it was a no-brainer and simple.

One thing they all had in common was that they had to learn to rest in his sovereignty. My prayer is that God has used this last month to encourage and enlighten you on what it looks like to rest in his sovereignty and how it is possible in your life.

Trusting in someone outside ourselves takes time. Some people never learn to trust God. Many children of Israel never learned to trust God. It seemed that God could never do enough to earn their trust. An entire generation perished in the wilderness and never experienced the promised land because they could not trust him.

Throughout our devotionals, we have seen how these Bible characters responded to God's sovereignty. No, they were not robots or puppets, whose every choice was determined by a sovereign God; they were people with the free will to choose their course of action. In every case, we have seen how God's sovereignty never negates or trumps the free will of man.

God made us in his likeness, and one mark of that likeness is our free will. We hear God say, "Whosoever will, let him come" (Mark 8:34, author paraphrase). We know through bitter experience the woe of an unsurrendered will and the blessedness or terror that may hang upon our choices. The reason for all this is the sovereign right of God to call saints and determine human destinies. The master choice is his; the secondary choice is ours. Salvation is, from the human side, a choice; from the divine side, it is a seizing-upon God. Our "accepting" and "willing" are reactions rather than actions.[33]

The question is: Does the Bible teach divine sovereignty or human freedom? The answer is yes. A careful reading of the Bible reveals that the writers of Scripture did not feel those two truths were contradictory, for they affirm them side by side without any attempt to explain them. They believed God was in control and that people must decide. Both truths are affirmed.[34]

Before we consider our last devotional, let me show you three Bible passages that lay the groundwork for today. The first one is found in John 6:44, where Jesus said, "No one can come to me unless the Father who sent me draws him, and I will raise him up on the last day." God takes the initiative. He calls us and draws us, which means a person cannot be saved whenever they want to but when God draws them to himself. God draws, yet some are not included, for they choose to reject his call.

The second passage is in John 12:32, where Jesus said, "As for me, if I am lifted up from the earth I will draw all people to myself." Here he tells us that he calls "all people," not "some people," not "all the elect," but clearly, he draws "all people" to himself. Some of those called decide to crown him while others decide to crucify him.

The third passage is in 2 Peter 3:9, where Peter tells us that Jesus "is patient with you, not wanting any to perish but all to come to repentance." God is an "equal opportunity" convictor who, in drawing all to himself, makes it possible to make a true decision to accept or reject Jesus.[35]

Yesterday we saw how Jesus came to reveal God the Father, but why? Why would Jesus step out of heaven, temporarily setting aside some of his divine attributes, as Paul mentions in Philippians 2:5–11, to come to earth to reveal his Father to us? Perhaps to show us he was real? Perhaps to show us what a sovereign God he is? There was a greater reason for revealing God the Father to us. Jesus revealed the Father to redeem the fallen. In other words, Jesus had redemption in his heart and mind as he came revealing the Father to us. That was his Father's work and will.

Jesus tells us in John 4:34, "My food is to do the will of him who sent me and to finish his work." Jesus's statement raises two questions. First, whose work was he sent to finish? The answer: God the Father's work. Second, what was the work he was sent to finish? The answer: the work of redemption. Jesus came to do the Father's work of redeeming lost humanity to himself.

Paul spoke of that work in 1 Timothy 2:5–6: "For there is one God and one mediator between God and mankind, the man Christ Jesus, who gave himself as a ransom for all." Jesus and his sacrifice on the cross bring sinful people and God together. He is God's only plan for salvation. Jesus said in John 14:6–7, "I am the way, the truth, and the life. No one comes to the Father except through me. If you know me, you will also know my Father. From now on you do know him and have seen him." Without Jesus, there is no going to heaven. Without Jesus, there is no knowing how to get to heaven. And without Jesus, there is no living in heaven.

We must all choose whether we will accept and obey the gospel or turn away in unbelief. Our choice is our own, but the consequences of the choice have already been determined by the sovereign will of God, and from this there is no appeal.[36]

Today's Prayer: *Lord, thank you for this thirty-day journey and the truths about your sovereignty I have discovered. I acknowledge and welcome your sovereign rule over my life. I'm grateful for the free will you have given me to choose to obey and follow you or to disobey and flee from you. Today, I choose to obey and follow you for the rest of my life. Come into my life and forgive me of my sins, as I turn from my sin and follow you as my Lord and Savior. In Jesus's name, amen.*

NOTES

1. Adrian Rogers quote found at https://www.goodreads.com/quotes/ 338345-a-faith-that-hasn-t-been-tested-can-t-be-trusted#:~:text=Quote%20by%20 Adrian%20Rogers%3A%20%E2%80%9CA,can't%20be%20trusted.%E2% 80%9D.

2. Malcolm Muggeridge quote found at https://gracequotes.org/quote/ contrary-to-what-might-be-expected-i-look-back-on-experiences-that-at-the-time-seemed-especially-desolating-and-painful-with-particular-satisfaction-indeed-i-can-say-with-complete-truthfulness-tha/.

3. J. Sidlow Baxter, *Majesty: The God You Should Know* (San Bernardino, CA: Here's Life Publishers, 1984), 26.

4. Cited in Os Guinnes, *The Call: Finding and Fulfilling the Central Purpose of Your Life* (Nashville, TN: Word, 1998), 165.

5. Steven J. Cole, "Cultivating Contentment," Lesson 53: Hebrews 13:5–6, Bible.org, accessed May 8, 2023, https://bible.org /seriespage/lesson-53-cultivating-contentment-hebrews-135-6.

6. Charles Spurgeon quote found in "He Preached a Big God with a Broken Heart: Charles Spurgeon (1834–1892)," desiringgod.org.

7. Baxter, *Majesty*, 33.

8. Author unknown.

9. Joseph Thayer, ed., *Thayer's Greek-English Lexicon of the New Testament* (Carol Stream, IL: Hendrickson Academic, 1995).

10. Cleon L. Rogers Jr. and Cleon L. Rogers III, *The New Linguistic and Exegetical Key to the Greek New Testament* (Grand Rapids, MI: Zondervan, 1998).

11. *Oxford Advanced American Dictionary*, 7th ed. (Oxford University Press, 2005), s.v. "inspiration."

12. Oswald Chambers, *Spiritual Leadership* (Chicago, IL: Moody Publishers, 2007), 117.

13. A. W. Tozer, *The Pursuit of Man* (Camp Hill, PA: Christian Publications, 1978), 41.

14. A. W. Tozer, *The Knowledge of the Holy* (San Francisco, CA: Harper Publishers, 1978), 1.

15. Mark Batterson, *In a Pit with a Lion on a Snowy Day* (Grand Rapids, MI: Multnomah Publishers, 2006), 32.

16. Herbert Lockyer, *All the Divine Names and Titles in the Bible* (Grand Rapids, MI: Zondervan, 1975), 24.

17. *The Spurgeon Study Bible* (Nashville: Holman Bible Publishers, 2017), 753.

18. William Hendriksen, *The Gospel of Luke* (Grand Rapids, MI: Baker Book House, 1978), 172.

19. Charles R. Swindoll, *Three Steps Forward Two Steps Back: Persevering through Pressure* (Nashville, TN: Thomas Nelson, 1980), 62.

20. R. T. Kendall, *The Thorn in the Flesh: Hope for All Who Struggle with Impossible Conditions* (Lake Mary, FL: Charisma House Publishing, 2004), 42.

21. Erwin W. Lutzer, *Failure: The Back Door to Success* (Chicago, IL: Moody Press, 1975), 127.

22. C. S. Lewis, *The Screwtape Letters* (San Francisco, CA: HarperOne, 2015).

23. Max Lucado, *Glory Days: Living Your Promised Land Life Now* (Nashville, TN: Thomas Nelson, 2015), 112.

24. Robert Robinson, "Come Thou Fount of Every Blessing," 1758, public domain.

25. A. W. Tozer, *The Knowledge of the Holy* (San Francisco, CA: Harper and Row, 1961), 117–18.

26. J. Oswald Sanders, *Spiritual Leadership* (Chicago, IL: Moody Publishers, 2007), 163.

27. C. S. Lewis, "Lewis to Arthur Greeves" (December 24, 1930), *The Letters of C. S. Lewis* (San Francisco, CA: HarperOne, 2017), 398–99.

28. J. C. Ryle, *Old Paths* (Edinburgh, GB: CrossReach, 2017), 159.

29. Phillip Yancey and Tim Stafford, *Secrets of the Christian Life* (Grand Rapids, MI: Zondervan, 1981), 110.

30. John Edmund Haggai, *Lead On! Leadership that Endures in a Changing World* (n.p.: Kobrey Press, 2006), 26.

31. Donald T. Phillips, *Lincoln on Leadership: Executive Strategies for Tough Times* (New York and Boston: Business Plus Publishers, 1992), 108.

32. John MacArthur, *Twelve Unlikely Heroes* (Nashville:, TN Thomas Nelson, 2012), 39–40.

33. A. W. Tozer, *The Pursuit of Man: The Divine Conquest of the Human Heart* (Camp Hill, PA: Christian Publications, 1950), 39.

34. Fisher Humphreys and Paul E. Robertson, *God So Loved the World: Traditional Baptists and Calvinism* (New Orleans, LA: Insight Press, Inc., 2000), 69.

35. Humphreys and Robertson, *God So Loved the World*, 74.

36. A. W. Tozer, *The Knowledge of the Holy* (New York, NY: Harper and Row, 1961), 120.